THE VANISHED GARDENS OF CORDOVA

ROSES

HIBISCUS

GERANIUMS

LILIES

JASMINE

LAVENDER

AZALEA

LOTUS

ROSEMARY

ORANGE BLOSSOM

DAISIES

POPPIES

BY EMIL■REM

—**Books by Emil Rem**—
Chasing Aphrodite
Heart of New York
The Vanished Gardens of Cordova

Book Design and Illustrations by Lorie Miller Hansen
Digital ePub design and creation by Andrea Cinnamond

9 781775 126683 >

First Edition, printed December 2023
www.EmilRem.ca   •   www.EICAPress.ca

"I will soothe you and heal you,
I will bring roses.
I too have been covered with thorns."

—Rumi—

EICA
PRESS

—TABLE OF CONTENTS—

I shoulda listened to mum...

"Son," she said. "Stop dreaming of becoming a writer. Be an accountant. You'll always have a job and pay your bills."

At the tender age of 60, I decided to rebel. Now I'm miserable and broke. Why? Because I allowed writing to possess me.

It's a woeful addiction. And there's no Writers Anonymous to turn to.

On its completion, Vanished Gardens brought a whoop of joy from me. It became my third opus. Warm climes, ancient sites, quirky characters all enchant me. I wrote about a summer family holiday spent in England, Gibraltar and Andalusia, Spain.

My vignettes always compare and contrast the present to the past, mainly through characters I meet and those once met. To contrast against the bleak Heart of New York, this, my third book *Vanished Gardens,* was meant to regale you with humour. Instead, once again, the writing took over and demanded its own direction.

> *"The moving finger writes; and, having writ, moves on: nor all*
> *thy piety nor wit shall lure it back to cancel half a line,*
> *nor all thy tears wash out a word of it."*

— Omar Khayyam —

Vanished Gardens took on the role of bittersweet memories—the struggle to survive and escape the world of accounting and our last family trip together. One after another, the stories became a giddy rollercoaster of amusement one moment, pathos the next. I, like my readers, had no clue where the writing would take me. But the takeaway was always a silver lining—no matter how outrageous were the slings and arrows of fortune, sunshine always prevailed.

May sunshine prevail upon you too, and gratitude overcome you at the end.

Emil

Emil Rem — Calgary, Alberta, October 23, 2023

"Khan's was suddenly eclipsed in darkness. A bright-red double-decker had come to rest in front of the restaurant's large windows, blotting out the sun."

CHAPTER 1

A TABLE FOR TWO AT KHAN'S

"**HURRY UP LEX**, we're late," he whispered.

While his wife Laura and his younger son Chris slept, pole-axed by jet lag, his older son Alex was wide awake, gazing out of the window of the London Heathrow Ariel Hotel. Aeroplanes took off and landed at Heathrow airport beneath a vibrant, sunny, cloudless sky—as it should have been on a balmy morning in late June.

Each year, he and his family flew in from Canada about this time, spending a couple of days in London to recuperate before upping their tent to other parts of Europe—this trip, they were on their way to Spain via Gibraltar.

Now was his time to spend a day alone with his son, a treat seldom available in the past six years as Alex studied his way up at The University of British Columbia (UBC) in Vancouver, on the other side of the Rockies from Calgary—his ever-fading home. In May, Alex had graduated and promptly landed a job there. It would begin in a few weeks from now, putting an end to their summers together. A bittersweet blow to his father, making today's trip to the heart of London so special.

He hadn't known what to expect at his son's graduation ceremony six weeks earlier. The whole family drove from Calgary to cheer him on. Even Chris turned out in a suit and tie.

Thousands of graduates filed through one after the other for hours at a time. At last, it was Alex's turn. The three of them from Calgary were led up never-ending flights of stairs at the back of the auditorium, so far away. They couldn't see the faces on stage below without opera glasses. How could Alex see them or know where they were? Laura wept at the futility of taking photos.

Now, here they were camped on the outskirts of London.

Alex turned from the window, tucked his iPhone into his pocket and followed him out the door to the front of the hotel to catch their free bus to the nearest underground tube station.

The bright red, double-decker was so packed that they had to fight their way to the back, only to find standing room. They could have been in the middle of New Delhi. East Indians surrounded them, mostly women with a sprinkling of their menfolk in turbans. Here and there, token members of the Caribbean community sat. In this melee, situated in the capital of Great Britain, besides the bus driver, there were no whites. Except for a fleck of flashy turbans and one or two gleaming gold rings decorating some of the women's noses, there was no colour anywhere. Only the drab, grubby sea-grey of their overalls. There was no luggage stashed to the ceiling of the storage area and no sign of wayward tourists on their way to their mecca in the city. The whole ensemble of passengers must have quit their shift at the same time to seek salvation on board.

He felt a curious affinity toward them. Decades ago, his mum fled the shame of divorce, landing on these shores, seeking sanctuary and sustenance for herself and her five-year-old son. With no formal education and only a smattering of garbled English, she too sought her fortune in countless hours and double shifts of mindless toil, ever grateful—for a chance to survive the day, for a chance to educate her son and help him elude the fate she couldn't. Her worn, young face was reflected in every frown and cast down eye of exhaustion displayed by workers around him.

At six-foot-two, Alex stood comfortably balanced, holding onto a safety strap with one hand, while manipulating his phone with the other. His unfortunate father—almost a foot shorter—had to stand on tiptoe to grab the adjacent strap dangling from the ceiling, all the while inspecting his watch in agitation. The bus swayed back and forth, thrusting him first into the person in front of him, then back-ward into the one behind. He offered an apologetic smile. Once he almost fell into the lap of a dozing female, her face enveloped in a veil, drifting off to sleep. She barely stifled a screech. Their bus skirted around the perimeter of the airport past aeroplanes embla-zoned with the decals of every airline in the world. Colour that was missing within the bus was more than compensated for by the garish tails and fuselages laying idle for the moment on the tarmac.

Twenty minutes later, the driver deposited them at Hatton Cross tube station.

Following the stampede of commuters into the station, they found the ticket office closed. The narrow channels to the trains were blocked off by gates—only to be opened by pressing a ticket through a designated slot. But there was nowhere to get the ticket. As father fretted, walking mindlessly up and down the corridor, Alex dis-appeared, returning a few minutes later with a peak-capped, red and navy-blue attired attendant in tow.

"The office is closed due to budget cuts. Come, I'll show you how to use the ticket machine."

They followed the attendant around the corner to a ticket kiosk they never would have found on their own. He shook his head.

Tickets in hand, they eventually made their way down some stairs to the platform, double-checking they were on the right one. Each minute, there was a rush of air and a swoosh of noise as trains halted briefly before flying off to the airport. Lights on the LED information board blinked on and off continuously to keep patrons up to date.

Within minutes, a train arrived to whisk them off to London, an hour's ride away.

At first, there was no dark tunnel to traverse. The tube acted as a regular train, passing above ground through one community and another, seeming to run parallel to the route his mother would take him on as a boy. In those days, he never had a say on the itinerary from Maidenhead, a few miles from where they had embarked today. As a boy, he dreaded those endless rounds to annual sales for clothes on Oxford Street. Today, he was the parent taking his own son out.

Across the aisle, chock-a-block with travellers, Alex was engrossed in his own world, his earbuds screwed tightly on, and his eyes glued to his phone. How could he explain all his hopes to his son, seemingly adrift on his own boat, or point out the sights and landmarks still standing from his childhood? The chug-along noise was deafening. He could hardly see Alex through the swaying mass of passengers standing between them.

As the tube juddered on its way, he noticed the passengers had changed from those on the bus. The train was just as packed, but with tourists from all over the world talking to their travel companions in every tongue as proclaimed in the Bible. More luggage lay across the aisles and doorways than passengers seated or standing. The haute-coutured plonked into ill-fitting seats beside 'hippie' students wearing Levi's with more holes than cloth made him smile. What were they trying to express? The discomfort they must feel with each other. The noise of travel was overbearing, as was the contrasting scent of rich, cloying Arabic perfume immixed with the sweat of travel and the stench of rotted food.

Alex was dressed in plain black cotton trousers with ne'er a hole or slash showing. A thin grey silk sweater hung over them. His feet sported a pair of white-soled runners—plimsolls his father would have called them. For once his hair was cropped short, instead of its usual long, tangled mess. To his father's continued annoyance, Alex wore a black baseball cap with white lettering spelling BRIXTON. In the England of his youth, Brixton was a tawdry district of London, infamous for its centuries-old prison for petty criminals—the last place anyone would want to be associated with. As a child, he was trained to take his cap off when indoors. He'd never seen Alex without it, even when in bed studying. Why Alex shunned colours baffled him. For his graduation, he had bought a beautiful dark blue suit for his son, spending a fortune on a fuchsia pink Hermès tie imprinted with tiny silver elephants to match his powder-blue shirt. Much to his chagrin, Alex chose to wear a tartan plaid tie in white, black and emerald green.

Alex finally took off his earbuds and tucked his phone away. His father leaned over, his whisper turning into a shout. "Are you hungry?"

The boy nodded.

"Khan's?"

Alex returned a crooked smile. It was an inside joke. Of course, they would dine at Khan's, off Bayswater—as they did every summer.

The tube rumbled on. Peering through the window, he noticed one row of dwellings after another, only broken up by townsites. Where were the villages and endless open fields he had travelled through as a boy on the same route?

Suddenly, all went dark as they descended into the underworld on the final stage to the city centre.

They escaped the underground at Queensway, scampering up the final two flights of stairs to hit the street.

The neighbourhood was a warren of tiny restaurants one after the other, interlaced with even tinier tobacconists and one or two impromptu mum and pop grocery stores. Their shop windows were scarcely wider than their single door entries—with one exception —Whiteleys.

A three-storey, white marbled Edwardian edifice completed in 1911, Whiteleys sprawled across an entire block, showering its patrons with large, beautiful bay windows to display its wares. Its roof was crowned with small, round-domed turrets flying the Union Jack. In contrast to the seedy establishments of its neighbours, the building drew a surfeit of pleasure from passersby. In its heyday, London's first department store rivalled Harrods and Liberty's. The store now long gone, the building was rebirthed into a shopping centre with a multi-cinema complex on its uppermost floor.

"Just a minute, Lex." He executed a U-turn, tugging his son along with him. Through the imposing carved wooden doors he barged, crossing the black and white checkered marble floors to a tiny corner store—the Feng-Shui shop. Run by a Chinese family, it sold every possible book on oriental culture. He found what he had been searching for in vain for years—Theodora Lau's Handbook of Chinese Horoscopes. There it was! Having paid, the two parted ways for half an hour—Alex, searching for a specific pair of runners for his brother, while his father crossed the mall to Marks and Spencer.

Twice a year when he was boy, on his birthday in June and at Christmas, his mother would treat him to the food emporium at Marks. There would always be a limit of what he could purchase. Before reaching the pay station, his mother would count the price of each item, sometimes twice, for fear of buying an amount beyond what she could afford. Today, unleashed from her deemed tyranny, he filled his basket with a dozen varieties of crisps—roast chicken flavoured, prawn cocktail, papadom, and Mexican sour cream. He splashed out on chocolates of every kind, mini containers of fresh English trifle, and cheese savouries.

Coming out of the store, with time to spare, he sat on a bench in the atrium, gazing up at the gallery of each floor. A pang of guilt hit him. He had not even totalled up the cost of his purchases, handing his credit card to the cashier and signing his receipt without demur. He wondered what his mother, now dead, would have said or what lessons his son would gather and take away with him of his spendthrift ways. Alex was skipping down the wide, concave marble stairs, an oversized bag swinging from his hand.

Exiting Whiteleys, father and son turned the corner and entered Khan's.

The familiar smell of spices, fried onions and burnt garlic welcomed them in. Despite the smell, Khan's reminded him inexplicably of a hospital ward run by Florence Nightingale in Turkey during the Crimean War. The dining room was large with pale, pastel-blue walls and long tables covered in white disposable paper that, to him, resembled primitive operating tables. The room was completely empty, marking the hiatus between the lunch-time and the supper crowd. On hearing the bell—triggered by their opening the door—a waiter hurried out of the kitchen and beckoned them to a table. They chose to sit beside a large, oversized window where he could gaze out onto the busy street overlooking Westbourne Grove.

There was no need to ask Alex what he wanted to order. Their annual visits always started with mango lassi with papadoms, vegetable pakoras, slivers of onion, spinach and potatoes mixed with cilantro, cumin, turmeric and salt, deep-fried in a batter of chick-pea flour. They ordered a plate of shish kebabs with freshly baked garlic naans as starters which were accompanied by a round indented brass salver of chutneys and pickles. They dolloped thick, sweet, golden mango chutney or watery, yet pungently sour, dark brown tamarind sauce into the cracks of half-bitten pakoras—just as he had done on his first visit here as a child with his Indian mother.

Staring at Alex in between bites, he wondered who this stranger was across from him.

"When you were born, you weighed just under five pounds. Did you know that? You missed being taken into ICU by a whisker."

Alex busied himself stuffing more Indian nourishment into his mouth. Once he finished eating his final morsel of pakora, he took a moment's breath before replying. "Mum's told me that story a hundred times."

"The doctor and social workers would call regularly. 'How's Alex eating?' They were constantly weighing you. You were in the lowest percentile for two years. They got mum so worried, she insisted you share our bed to keep an eye on you. Then she worried I would roll over and suffocate you. Now I get a neck ache looking up at you. What went wrong?" he jibed. "Funny thing. You never cried. I remember waking up in the middle of the night. Your mum was in her rocking chair breastfeeding you. Once you'd had your fill, you smiled like an angel."

"Dad. Please." Alex rolled his eyes.

Taking advantage of the lull in Alex twiddling with his phone, he asked, "In all those five years at UBC, what did you learn?"

"What do you mean what did I learn? I got two degrees."

All those years of talking about the humdrum—the logistics of transferring money or the latest movies seen—they had never talked of values or the philosophy of living. How each was faring with his work associates or friends. It seemed impossible to enter into that realm now. He didn't know where to begin.

"Are you happy? Sometimes, we get carried away by our goals. Never have a moment to really appreciate what we have. To discover what makes us happy. I spent years in accounting after failing high school. I was determined never to fail again. On qualifying, I realized it wasn't what I wanted after all. By then it was too late. I was stuck. That's why we let you decide on your own path and not to pressure you into a career you didn't want. It's not that Mum and I weren't interested."

Alex stopped eating and looked up at him. "I'm really happy with the job I'm getting. I've made great friends, all the way through university. Vancouver's booming. There are plenty of opportunities in my field. I love what I do. You don't need to worry."

Khan's was suddenly eclipsed in darkness. A bright-red double-decker had come to rest in front of the restaurant's large windows, blotting out the sun, forcing him to reassess his surr-oundings. He appraised the room and its inhabitants. Thank goodness some things remained the same. The waiters of his childhood when he had forayed into the depths of this restaurant, pulling his mother behind him, had long gone, but the profile of their successors never changed: short, gaunt, cadaverous, dark-skinned and devout in pursuit of their duties. The current servers—still all men, could have been cloned from their predecessors. They hovered about their tasks in silence—except when spoken to—like an order of Benedictine monks fulfilling their vows.

As a child, entering this paradise for an hour, he had cast away the boiled potatoes and limp cauliflower of his English foster family and, with his Indian mother's connivance, ordered a veritable feast of the exotic. Returning to Khan's decades later, his choices off the menu were no different: aloo paratha (potato pancakes), Madrasi mutton curry with potato and peas pilau, golden-yellowed in saffron, garnished with slivers of boiled eggs. Steam rose from the brown sludge of curry, its lingering odour impregnated their clothes and hair, waiting to be detected by Laura on their return home. Like in the old days, once he had dished out the food onto his plate, the etiquette of knives and forks was thrown to the winds, replaced by his right hand shovelling curry on to the rice, rolling it into balls and feeding them into his mouth. Father and son savoured their meal in silence.

But he couldn't stay quiet for long. "What's this job about? Are you working for a union?"

"No. We were set up by the Union of Mayors of BC to help them communicate and coordinate with each other. Every year, we organize their annual convention. There're only five people working in my office. It's exactly what I wanted as a start." Alex tore off strips of naan, propelling them into shovels to eke out pieces of shish kebab.

"Do you know how lucky you are? In my work, I come across dozens of families whose kids have graduated from some of the top universities in Canada. And they're all jobless."

Perplexed, he wondered at how easily Alex had landed on his feet, so unlike his parents, who had entered the country as working immigrants and struggled ever since. Both had come from impoverished families barely able to survive. Neither dreamed that, in Canada, their son would attend a private school. At Delta West Academy, a colony of a hundred pupils encompassing Grade 1 to Grade 12, Alex thrived. There, he gravitated to making friends a grade or two above him—remarkable to his parents as he was the youngest in his class. As each grade led to the next, Alex's schooling seemed never-ending—but suddenly, he was in Grade 12 taking his final exams. It was then his parents realized how swiftly time had flown.

At Khan's, it was nearing three o'clock. An elderly couple were being quietly shown to their table. They were wearing heavy, threadbare, gaberdine coats—too warm for a summer's day. They wore no haute couture apparel, nor were they encumbered with oversized carrier bags emblazoned with the names of London's glitziest stores—the hallmark of the consummate tourist. He imagined them as impecunious relics of the good old British Empire, come home from the tropics to relish in their biennial furlough at the only remaining 'club' they belonged to, making their pilgrimage to the ever-vanishing past, as he was with his son.

"Remember the shock you gave us when you announced you were applying to UBC?"

Alex's phone rang. He had lost him again.

"Yes. Yes. OK. See you when you get back." The conversation ended, Alex turned his attention to his father again.

"Who was that?"

"One of my buddies from UBC. He's at Heathrow changing flights for Korea."

Who exactly was this buddy? Back in his son's schooldays in Calgary, he would have known his friend's name, their parents and everything else about them. Now father and son seemed to be oper-ating on different planets. He gave up, retreating to the normal mundane and pedestrian, enquiring, "Aren't those calls expensive?"

"We were on Messenger. It cost nothing."

A large Indian mahogany pendulum clock, hanging on a nearby wall, struck four. Khan's was inexorably filling up, its quiet lull replaced by an ascending hubbub of noise and conversation. Menu items were loudly discussed, the opinion of waiters sought. Food orders given, then rescinded, superseded by more inquiries and discussion.

The final course arrived—thick creamy mango kulfi downed with cinnamon and a brimming, richly sweet yet spicy, milky chai. They ate and sipped in silence, allowing the exuberance of the room and its patrons to wash over them. He mused over Alex, back to being engrossed in his communication tool of choice.

As his father sifted assiduously through the past, Alex was busying himself plotting out the future. Little by little, the two were drifting away from each other, like icebergs gently breaking apart, moving independently out to sea. Alex was filled with natural confidence—a quality sorely lacking in his father. He marvelled at the seeming ease with which Alex set and achieved his goals, while each day his father fought his own demons of doubt and fear. What instigated success? Education? Family support? The right contacts? The right opportunity at the right time? Or was it that inner belief so remarkably placed into his son's hands by whom, nobody knew? A gift so inordinately precious.

Their bill paid, father and son re-entered the world of blazing sunlight, Alex casually mounting his Oakley sunshades as his father struggled ineffectively to divert the sun from his watering eyes.

AUTHOR'S NOTE

There comes a moment when your six-year-old child, who has never grown up in your eyes, suddenly transmogrifies before you into a responsible adult.

It happened on our last trip together to Khan's.

Quite poignant as Khan's was a restaurant that my poor mum gravitated to, dragging her five -year-old son (me) once a year, until the time I left her in my mid-twenties to emigrate to Canada.

Poignancy took hold even before Alex and I reached our destination, in the form of East Indian manual labourers boarding our bus, reminding me instantly of the series of lowly jobs my mum had to grudge through, to allow me to escape her destiny.

Khan's itself hadn't changed much. On my first visit, I had just completed a Ladybird book about Florence Nightingale. The large, antiseptic room—its walls a pastel baby blue— harnessed myimagination to the hall of wounded in Scutari, where she and her volunteers nursed them. That memory stuck, to the last day with Alex.

ILLUSTRATOR'S NOTE

Travelling isn't only about new experiences—sometimes it's about reliving and passing on memories to your children— finding those little moments where generational bubbles overlap and seizing your opportunity to connect.

"It seemed like yesterday when Alex had been placed between the two protagonists, his tiny legs dangling precariously off the bench into thin air."

CHAPTER 2

PASSING THROUGH

HE RACED PAST Alex, his breath escaping him, clawing his way through the throng of tourists and emerged from Green Park underground station like a mole blinking in the harsh sunlight. And there it was, the centuries-old beloved vista of London Town. Not the tawdry brazenness of Piccadilly Circus, nor the arch-celebration-of-invincibility Trafalgar Square. Here lay his quintessential London.

Across the broad boulevard of Piccadilly, overburdened with endless traffic, despite restrictions, stood the black, ornate wrought-iron gates of Green Park. Through their lacquered railings, was a dirt path, originally for horses, stretching across the tranquil parkland and ponds (populated by swans and ducks) leading to Buckingham Palace. To the right stood a fruit stand, its occupier, a gnarled centenarian sporting a flat tweed cloth cap and covered from neck to ankle in an olive-green apron, selling punnets of strawberries, apricots and his childhood favourites, hairy green gooseberries—the sharpest tasting of all. To the left of the blackened gates stood the lofty Ritz, lording over its domain. To him, once also an immigrant to this kingdom, it was an inspiration that a Swiss hotelier could leave such a mark on British heritage. To his son, born as an equal in Canada, The Ritz presented an altogether different connotation. Alex had caught up, whisked his iPhone out and was busily snapping photos at every angle of the hotel and its frock-coated yeomen. Yet another quaint edifice to be taken pictures of and instantly transmitted to friends across the globe.

"Pops, I'm off to Ralph Polo. I'll meet you later."

What could he say? He shrugged and consulted his watch. "It's 4:30. How about meeting back at six? At Hatchards?"

Alex nodded. In the blink of an eye, he was gone, leaving his father to retrace their annual pilgrimage alone.

Words of an ancient and revered hymn, sung a thousand times at school morning assembly, rang out to him. *"And did the countenance divine, shine forth upon our clouded hills? And was Jerusalem builded here, Among the dark satanic mills?"*

He had been five when he arrived in England. An East Indian out of Africa, brought up by a working-class English family whose sole preoccupation was survival, not the propagation of British imperialism. Why they took on the horrendous and thankless task of nurturing and nourishing this strange, tiny, dark creature astonished him and the more so as he grew up and understood what the responsibility entailed when he married and begot off-spring of his own.

Taking his life into his own hands, he stepped onto the road, crossing Piccadilly toward the fruit stand.

The centenarian saw him coming and greeted him with a smile. "A punnet of gooseberries did yer saay ? 'Ere y'are. Five paands please."

Gazing at the man, he couldn't help asking, "How long have you been here?"

"Abaat a week." Seeing the consternation on his customer's face, he relented. "Na mate, bin here since the days of Queen Victoria, Gawd bless her." He winked.

He wondered if the costermonger knew that every year, Canada celebrated Queen Victoria's official birthday as a national holiday—something unheard of in England, where she reigned for almost a century as the greatest of her country's monarchs at the zenith of its world power. Curious how the ties of generations of imperial settlers bound them closer to Britannia than her own natives. There lay the juxtaposition of a colonial empire built, then relinquished.

From his early days as a child in England, the love of British greatness and tradition seeped insidiously into his psyche. On qualifying as an accountant, he moved to London, sharing the basement of a pied-a-terre overlooking Hyde Park. On weekends, he would explore a different district of the city, relishing each visit. He expected it to last forever. Alas, his time was cut short after only a few months. Economic calamity came in the wake of Margaret Thatcher. Made redundant, he was forced to return to his hometown of Maidenhead, before emigrating to Canada. Now Alex was badgering him to apply for a British passport so he could live and work in London. He was sure Alex would never be made redundant or succumb to sharing a basement flat in London. Alex lay claim to loftier goals than mere survival.

Was he any more comfortable in his role as a Canadian? While *1066 and All That*—the Norman conquest of England—was ingrained in him, he couldn't recall the number and names of the provinces comprising his adopted country. Decades later, he still subscribed to BBC World Service and the English Premier League, while shunning hockey, the lifeblood of his sons' interests. Like sponges, his boys absorbed every aspect of being Canadian, proud of the fact that they, like the multitude of their friends, descended from every corner of the world and were part of this great and wondrous land.

One summer, he had taken his family to visit Hong Kong.

"Pops, where's the Canadian embassy?"

"I don't know." Horror dawned on his face. "You haven't lost your passport, have you?"

"It's Canada Day tomorrow. Chris and I want to celebrate."

So much for England and its influence. They had become Canadian before his eyes. He was the last of his breed.

A tiny voice within him whispered, but they were always Canadian. Weren't they born and bred in Canada? Did they know any other life? Why such a sudden shock?

He had never had that sense of unquestioned belonging that his boys had, of being an indisputable part of the fabric of a nation. When he had lived in England, he dreamt of Africa, longing to be sent back home. In Canada, his mind stubbornly dwelt on England, mocking every triviality that his adopted country presented: from their Americanized language—elevators instead of lifts—to introducing themselves by their Christian names to strangers. After decades of living on the Prairies, he still felt constrained and uncomfortable, as if being forced to wear a gaudy flowered jacket that was too tight on the shoulders and much too long in the sleeves. It seemed his whole life had been spent in transit, from one community to the next, from one culture to another, forever observing, never committing fully.

Here in London, it was almost five. Enough time to visit his favourite sculpture on Bond Street.

Scoffing two gooseberries at a time, his eyes watering with their citric tang, he instinctively glanced over his shoulder to see if either of his mothers—natural or foster—were watching, then remembered they had been dead for years. Both would have been horrified to witness him eat in the street, never mind gobbling down unwashed berries.

The Allies Sculpture comprised a wooden bench stationed in front of Asprey, the renowned jeweller. It celebrated the special relationship between England and the USA during World War II. On that bench sat Churchill and Roosevelt petrified in bronze. The PM held a smoking cigar between his fingers as he levered himself off one corner, the rest of him leaned forward toward his friend. The President, sitting at the other end of the bench had the length of his arm resting on the back, smiling as though sharing a joke.

It seemed like yesterday when Alex had been placed between the two protagonists, his tiny legs dangling precariously off the bench into thin air. Today, there would be no way he could fit on the bench between the two—and his spindly legs would stretch along the pavement. Besides, nowadays, Alex shunned participating in family photos, yet his Facebook was full of images of himself surrounded with friends in activities ranging from barbeques to mountain climbing. He didn't mind Alex's aversion to family photos—he had hardly a handful of his own childhood. It was the happiness expressed in abundance that cut him. Perhaps he coveted the circle of friends Alex had assembled around him, an ability lost to his father as he negotiated from one unsettling environment to the next. As he established his life in Canada, he considered himself too old to risk opening up as he would have done at Alex's age.

The sculpture captured his heart—two friends caught in the midst of their daily confab. He missed Eric, his Scottish high school friend. It had been decades since they had last met. With the surname of Smith, his friend was impossible to track down. From an apocryphal (dodgy) source he learned Eric had migrated to Dubai, about the same time as he had left for Canada. He had never gone to university where opportunity arose to make lasting friends. In Canada, he had drifted out of public accounting within fifteen months. Gary, the only friend he had made there, died of a heart attack a few years later, ironically while preparing his tax returns.

Alex had attended a private school catering to students from Grades 1 to 12. He carried those friends with him still today. He collected two degrees from university. There, he remained for five years, once again accumulating steadfast friends from every corner of the world, remaining in touch daily through the internet and apps like Messenger. In his day, his father never had those means to retain far-dispersed friendships. Behind the satisfaction of a job well done in nurturing stability and opportunity in his son, that spectre of envy lurked intermingled with the fear of any future contribution made redundant.

Behind Churchill and Roosevelt stood Asprey, crown jeweller to the Royal Family for generations. It was here that Prince Charles purchased an engagement ring for Diana, his (at the time) future consort. Asprey displayed its wares in small, discrete window cabinets, jutting out from its white walls. He remembered his first visit here with Alex. His son standing on tiptoes, his hands clutching the window frame to gain a glimpse of the treasures within, still unable to see until his father lifted him upon his shoulders.

Today, the Aladdin's trove of precious gems and watches lay on maroon velvet beneath probing beams of light. Varicoloured diamonds and finger-sized green emeralds coruscated and enticed. Someone had mingled individual pearls—from milky white to stunning golden—headlong into a necklace of silky grey pearls. As Alex grew up, they would venture into the revered establishment pretending to buy a gift for his wife, Laura. Without Alex, he didn't have the audacity to enter Asprey and grandstand.

Time was running out. He still wanted to buy Alex a present. With that in mind, he jog-trotted two blocks and darted into Burlington Arcade.

Built in 1818, the arcade was one of London's first and finest shopping centres. The fifty-odd exclusive boutiques within were clustered along a narrow walk, barely eight feet wide, covered in a long series of V-shaped glass roofs. From one end to the other, the whole structure was supported by carved, white marble arches. But he had no time to marvel at its setting. A beadle, accoutred in top hat and dark frock coat overhung with miles of white brocade, eyed him cautiously as he glided past and into Vilebrequin, the world's master purveyor of swimwear. Sink or swim, he was determined to break Alex's mould of monochrome clothing. Vilebrequin was famous for the brightest and sharpest swimming trunks he had ever seen. One such had caught his eye in its window display—in shocking purple with iridescent tortoises in shades of mandarin orange and jade green. He gulped at the price. Well, if Alex didn't approve, he could always gift them to his brother.

A few minutes' walk along Piccadilly, sandwiched between a store selling hunting whips and an Italian bistro, stood his favourite book-store, Hatchards. It was like stepping into Dickens's Old Curiosity Shop. Its musty rooms were a warren of heavy dark wood, their portent magnified by ancient, shadowy lighting. He spotted the latest John le Carré offering—the title reading *The Pigeon Tunnel*. Alex would love it—one of the few interests they shared. As he handed over his Visa card, the wall clock chimed six and Alex entered—on time as always.

He wondered if his son had remembered him whilst shopping, as he had done. While leading his frenetic lifestyle, he wasn't sure if he ever thought of his father. It appeared the breeding and upbringing of children was passé—a thankless chore taken for granted by the very children on whom so much love, energy and time was lavished. He sighed, switching off his reverie as though turning off a radio, then turned smiling towards his son.

"Pops, look what I got you."

AUTHOR'S NOTE

The opening description of a costermonger remains my favourite, as does this chapter's ending.

ILLUSTRATOR'S NOTE

A fondly remembered moment can trigger vivid emotional reactions that bring you full circle—showing you all the ways you and your circumstances have changed and grown—what you've left behind and the important things you still keep close to your heart.

CHAPTER 3

THE OLD SCHOOL TRY

THEY HAD BEEN kept awake all night in their hotel room.

The London Heathrow Ariel Hotel was a white circular building. Kids screeched and charged round and round the corridor adopting it as their personal racetrack. How many times had he called reception and heard the same sweet Polish night auditor pleading for his tolerance and understanding?

"Our sincere apology. They are a large family from Saudi Arabia. They've taken all the other rooms on your floor and below. The children are all suffering from jetlag and can't sleep."

"Nor can we," he had retorted, dropping the phone and sandwiching his ears between two pillows.

He glanced over at Chris, his head hidden beneath a blanket. Lying beside him, Alex was still awake, riffling through *Time Out*, the London visitors' guide to where to go and what to see. Laura emerged from their bed like a zombie, heading straight for the bathroom, ignoring him completely.

The air hung heavy with smouldering resentment.

Their tiny room looked like a bomb had gone off. Dirty clothes mingled with clean ones, covering the one armchair in the room. The debris of iPhones, iPads, innumerable cables and chargers were strewn across the floor, almost wrecking the sole of his foot as he stepped out of bed. Half-empty packets of Marks and Spencer crisps spilled across the white counterpanes, laying unclaimed beside their companions of half-empty cans of pop, their fizz long expired. There was barely a foot space between one single bed and the other. Their luggage sat open to the world on any remaining floor space, belts emerging from them like uncoiling snakes of infinite colours. The extraordinarily tidy and ordered Laura had lifted not a finger to combat the chaos. The air was fuggy with the putrid odour of half-eaten food left unattended overnight.

It was all his fault. He had booked the room at the last minute during the busiest part of the tourist season, never considering any other hotel because he had patronised this one since a child in his mother's arms.

Never comfortable with booking online, the receptionist he called from Canada crooned, "Aah! Well sir, we only have one room available. And it is one of our smaller ones. Perhaps too small to accommodate a party of four?"

"We'll take it," he bellowed over the static. "We're only in for two nights. It can't be that small."

It was.

His watch showed 10 a.m. This was their last day in transit before leaving for Gibraltar early the next morning. He was not going to waste the day sleeping in nor in a surfeit of shopping—they could do that in Spain once they arrived. He had other plans.

Hertz Rentals stood across the road. The car lot stretched out for miles. The office itself was barely larger than a porter's lodge. Already at this hour, there were a dozen customers—all men, their clothes in various disarray—ahead of him. There was no chair for him to sit on. The few existing ones were sequestered by wives with kids galore and baggage in all shapes and sizes, dumped willy-nilly, one sliding off the other, the owners too tired to park them in any respectable order.

The air was rent with mothers commanding their wayward six-year-olds to stop running around. Too late. One had charged headlong into him eliciting a whoosh as all the air escaped his lungs. The sweltering heat within succeeded in releasing rivulets of sweat, steaming his glasses to uselessness. Through the fog, he glared at the beautiful movielike posters of the chic, perfectly coiffured, elegantly dressed males and females—so relaxed. He returned to the hell embroiling him.

When he eventually reached the front of the line he asked for an automatic drive.

"Sorry sir. We only have manuals left."

Having lived in Canada for decades and never having driven in England since, the manual drive became a further hindrance as did the roads, swollen with traffic speeding down the wrong side of the road.

Thankfully, his family was waiting dutifully for him on his return.

No sooner had they seated themselves, then the complaints started.

"Why is it so hot in here?"

"Because I don't know how to put on the aircon. I must have pressed the wrong button."

"Why are the windows steamed up. How can you see to drive?"

"Must have pressed the internal air recycle button. Don't know how to correct it."

The pint-sized car was as claustrophobic as their hotel room, as humid as a tropical jungle.

The car was not American, but some European make, probably manufactured in Bulgaria. The rental crew had no time to explain, and he had no time to ask. He was running late.

Laura helped herself to the handbook in the glove compartment. Ten minutes later she had adjusted all the settings back to normal.

Alex yawned and asked, "Where are we heading?", unwittingly launching an avalanche of recrimination.

"Burnham Grammar School."

"Birmingham WHAT?" the answering chorus rang.

"I thought we were going shopping?" Laura demanded.

"What about our trip to Greenwich?" came back Alex, still clutching his copy of Time Out.

"Burnham Grammar was my alma mater. I wasn't privileged like you to go to university."

"Po-opps," the boys crescendoed in disapproval. Laura remained ominously silent.

The hour-long drive along the Bath Road to Burnham Village took them past endless rows of tiny shops from newsagents to off-licences (liquor stores). Each vied with its neighbour to be smaller. Their exteriors were either untouched for decades with paint peeling off, once white, now tooth-stained yellow, or festooned with garish blue and white neon signs in indecipherable Hindi. Where once there had been village greens and commons, not a gap remained between one decrepit establishment and the next, from beginning to end. He cursed every roundabout, almost forgetting to enter on the left side and not the right. Meanwhile, his family had returned to their slumber.

They entered Burnham Village at the bottom of its High Street. In front lay the village green which had been shorn in half by the erection of a four-storey building at one end. The narrow, cobbled street was impassable. Cars parked on both sides hogged the road, blocking traffic in and out of the village.

"You'll have to go out of the village to park," a passerby advised.

A spot was eventually found halfway between the village and Burnham Grammar.

He roused his family and led Laura by the hand, his pace accelerating as he neared his former school. Suddenly, he ducked through a narrow pathway covered on all sides by hedgerows and finally found what he was searching for—the iron side gate he used decades ago to enter surreptitiously when arriving late. It was padlocked, rusty and overgrown with roots and branches. He steered them back to the front entrance.

The extensive grounds and buildings hadn't changed at all. They were as imposing as ever. A long drive led to the main entrance of the building. To the right lay acres of manicured lawns resplendent with a field hockey pitch in front. Its spotless white boxed goals glimmered in the sunlight. Football fields rested beyond. The large assembly hall decked in floor-to-ceiling windows blinded them with reflected sunlight as they approached. His family remained eerily silent as though sleepwalking.

Enrolment to this grammar school was part of his Indian mother's master plan to see him accepted at Oxford or Cambridge, just as it was taking back her son from the working-class English family who had fostered him for a dozen years. In her mind it would lead him to a life of privilege and social acceptance which she could never achieve. It would bypass the strugle and turmoil she had faced daily since her arrival.

His mother didn't realise the awe and dread this white-walled, immaculately-lawned institution engendered in him from the very start. How it drained him of any personal initiative, of any sense of belonging. It wasn't just the starched uniform he had to squeeze into. His former school was no more than a tumbled-down house made of flint in the poorest part of town. It welcomed thirty pupils in all. North Town Primary School was a comfortable ten-minute walk from his foster parents' home. To reach the new school he had to take two buses and inevitably, from time to time, caught the wrong one in his panic to arrive on time. From a member of a community of thirty, he was plunged into a sea of six hundred pupils, all clone-like in their official uniforms. How was he ever expected to fit in, let alone excel in this environment? Even now, thirty years later, his throat tightened as he felt that old school tie chafe his neck again.

His trance-like submission at the start of his seven years at Burnham Grammar was shattered by two serendipitous incidents.

Incident One—A bully confronted him...

Not a common student, but the Assistant Headmaster—one Mr. Thomas Waller—who would twist your ear and mete out countless detentions if he didn't like you.

He broke off his reverie only to witness his family following him in sullen silence.

"Chris, see that large hall to the left of the main entrance?" he pointed. "That was our canteen. We had to line up to be served lunch. I refused to eat."

This great hall housing a hundred tables—each seating eight—was larger than the whole of his previous school. As the lunch bell rang, they were herded through glass doors, hurried to the front to form a line to be served by women behind their counter, uniformed in white pinafores and turbaned hair. Behind the servers, who had just that minute disposed of their duty as cooks and chefs, lay the kitchen, its shutters opened to reveal a battalion of steel equipment and vast trolleys transporting containers of food to the front. A myriad of aromas attacked the newly arrived participants, from the tang of freshly made gravy to the smell of custard already poured and congealing in miniature bowls of over-stewed apple. The cacophony of trundling trolleys was overpowered by the hubbub of pupils and teachers in a room that a few minutes before had been devoid of all sound and motion.

Lunches were ghastly. The odour of pilchards in tomato sauce impregnated his memory. He was a Muslim and not permitted to eat pork. The school served liberal doses of Spam. At the time, he was the only Muslim in the school. There were no rules to deal with religious minorities and their dietary requirements. So, he simply refused to eat.

He turned to Laura and his boys for sympathy. There was none, only simmering hostility.

"My mum was well off by then. She would splurge money on me every week. As she worked three jobs a week, I had to feed myself when I was with her.

Here in Burham Village, two sisters ran The Copper Kettle restaurant and they specialized in all the foods that Flo, my English mother, used to cook and have ready for me on my return from school."

Remembering the sisters' roast beef and Yorkshire pudding took him back to his English family's Sunday lunches. He could still see the steam rising from gravy poured onto his beef and hear the resounding crunch of the Yorkshire pudding. And just as Flo had sat with him after school while he ate, interested to hear how his day had been, the two sisters had taken turns sitting beside him to chat.

He tried to reach out to his sons again. "Mr. Waller soon heard of my refusal to eat and placed me daily at his table. He'd make me sit until everyone else had finished. By that time my lunch break was over. Ended up with detention for a year before Mr. Waller gave up. But you know what happened? I became popular at school. Mr. Waller was about as loved as the school lunches. No one had ever stood up to him before."

Alex remained unimpressed. "What was the point? Why couldn't you eat just a little? There must have been something you could have taken? Why create such a fuss?"

"Because you don't let others bully you into something you don't want." Chris had finally woken up.

Back in Canada, Alex never argued with his teachers. In return, he always got what he wanted including all the annual students' accolades. Chris complained about everything and got none.

"Looking back, perhaps I should have followed your advice. It would have been so convenient and saved all these detentions," he murmured. Laura remained silent in apparent agreement.

The confession of perhaps taking a convenient course in life niggled him. His English parents, rich as paupers, should never have provided him a shelter for a dozen years without reward. They could barely feed themselves, let alone take in some dark waif who stuck out like a sore thumb in their poverty-stricken, bellicose council house community. If they had taken the convenient course, where would he have landed in life? And, for that matter, his two sons?

Deciding to retract his previous statement and remonstrate, he turned, only to find the boys had disappeared.

"They're over there inspecting those wooden goals," mumbled Laura petulantly.

Chris returned. "Pops, what kinda sport is that?" he asked, pointing. "And why have planks of wood around the goals?"

"The wood's there to protect the netting. To stop the small heavy balls from puncturing it. It's for field hockey. That's where I discovered my talent for sport."

"What talent?" the boys yelped.

"I wasn't always this short, fat, hairy guy puffing his way up stairs. Right Hon?" He turned to Laura for confirmation. There was none, as she was still brooding over her lost shopping and sightseeing.

Incident Two—He became an athlete...

In the Lower Sixth, his penultimate year at school, his class was given a choice of playing sports on Friday afternoons or taking needlework and domestic science such as cooking. He was the only boy to choose the latter. Firstly, he was hopeless at sport. Secondly, to thumb his nose at Mr. Waller, who ranted that needlework wasn't offered as an excuse to avoid gruelling cross-country running for two hours.

On that placid Friday afternoon, he was resting on the edge of a large table in the needlework and tailoring room, his legs dangling in the air, chattering away. The large room hosted a dozen females and him. Despite its size and clinical stark white walls with ne'er a notice or poster in sight, the room breathed a sense of peace and relaxation— until Mr. Whitcombe, the P.E. master, barged his way in.

"Get your shorts on. You're playing hockey."

"I don't have any kit. Besides..."

"Tough. Find some." Mr. Whitcombe had no time for excuses. "By the way, you're playing centre-forward so make sure you score at least a dozen goals."

It was the end of the football season and the beginning of hockey. At Burnham Grammar, the same boys who played in the First XI football team, by their proven prowess, also played in the hockey First XI. That day, the two matches overlapped. The football match against a prominent visiting team took precedence over hockey, leaving them one man short.

How life changes in the blink of an eye. One minute he was idly gossiping with the girls, the next minute he was at the centre of the pitch surrounded by hunks much bigger than him.

As the match progressed, it dawned on him that he wasn't so hopeless after all. His position was perfect. He didn't have to run around winning the ball back from the opposition. All he had to do was find space and wait for a pass. His small frame combined with his low centre of gravity—he weighed a hundred pounds and rose to five foot four inches—was perfect for bending down to manoeuvre his stick. All the fastest players were attackers. The defenders he faced were slow and heavy. He could outrun and bypass them with ease. Soon, he began to enjoy himself. Before half-time he scored. His second followed before the final whistle. At the end of the match, he was permanently installed in the First XI, becoming highly popular and finally beginning to love his school.

None of this mattered to his family who appeared beyond bored.

They reached the hallowed school's entrance. Matron's office had been replaced by a large reception stage barring any further progress. A tall girl in her twenties stood up to greet them.

"I'm an old schoolboy returning from Canada. Can we come in and see the school?"

She demurred. "Sorry, sir. Security doesn't permit. All tours have to be booked two weeks in advance."

As she spoke, a bell clanged across the school. Hundreds of pupils stormed down the corridor beyond, some wading against the tide, others being carried along, scampering upstairs to their awaiting classrooms for their next period. He too was carried along with that tide to decades old memories of panic, trying to fully comprehend that there was no longer one teacher for all subjects and only one room to sit in. Each class had its own room and teacher. He had withstood the test of his first days, ever planning ways of escape.

Yet, here he was begging entry once more.

He returned to the perfect receptionist dressed in tweed, making her look so much older, wearing tortoiseshell glasses to further emphasise her staid and traditional role.

"Alright then. Can we at least walk the grounds?"

She declined. "So sorry. Security..." She was crestfallen but tied inextricably to the protocols given her.

So much for a happy reunion.

Chris tugged his shirt. "Pops, can we go eat? We didn't have breakfast and it's past one o'clock."

Laura stepped in, her voice softening. "Never mind, Hon. Why don't we walk back to the village where we can eat? You may meet someone you know."

They beat a retreat, the boys overtaking them, walking swiftly toward the High Street.

Suddenly, he heard Chris shouting to his brother. "Quick. Look here."

Now what?

Two doors up the high street, a large white sandwich board stuck out onto the road. Its deep blue lettering welcomed you to Akash Royal Indian Restaurant.

A large neon sign blazed O-P-E-N in blinking, flaming-orange glory.

The boys rushed over, galvanised into life, snapping one photo after another with their iPhones.

Akash was the name of their best friend at school. They were transmitting their takes to him and their circle of buddies.

As fast as the boys entered the restaurant, they rushed back out again to collect their parents.

Steps away from entering, he let go of Laura's hand and paused, searching up and down the row of Tudor cottages and shops. Where was the Copper Kettle? It had been around here somewhere. Then it dawned on him. He nodded to himself, observing his family wryly in their hurry—none of them realised that the Akash had usurped his beloved restaurant—his haven each evening after school.

AUTHOR'S NOTE

And did those feet in ancient time
walk upon England's mountains green?
And was the holy Lamb of God
on England's pleasant pastures seen?
And did the countenance divine
shine forth upon our clouded hills?
And was Jerusalem buildéd here
Among these dark satanic mills?

Bring me my bow of burning gold!
Bring me my arrows of desire!
Bring me my spear! O clouds, unfold!
Bring me my chariot of fire!

I will not cease from mental fight,
nor shall my sword sleep in my hand,
till we have built Jerusalem
in England's green and pleasant land.

As I step-marched down the driveway of my old Burnham Grammar School, my family in tow, the ancient hymn 'Jerusalem' rattled my frame. Morning school assemblies imbued in me the glory of what Great Britain had once been—even though, as an East Indian I would never have risen beyond the state of a faithful manservant.

I looked to converting the Philistines behind me, to no avail. My only foe to vanquish was the boredom in their eyes.

The glazed look writ large upon their faces only disappeared when they came across an Indian Restaurant in the village, The Akash—the name of their best friend at school.

No-one saw me weep for the old traditional restaurant run by two English sisters, steamrolled over by this gaudy, oriental eaterie.

ILLUSTRATOR'S NOTE

You can laugh or you can cry—or both! It's not easy to explain to people who weren't there about pivotal events that threatened to break your spirit, but became instead, character building moments of triumph or comfort.

CHAPTER 4

MONKEY BUSINESS

HE YAWNED AS he made himself more comfortable on their spacious queen-sized bed. The newly renovated suite was a far cry from the tiny closet of a room they had left behind in London. Was that only a few hours ago? It seemed more like a week.

As he snuggled into his oversized pillow, Laura asked, "Hon, can you open the balcony window? It's a little stuffy in here."

He pushed, then pulled the lever on the sill to no avail. Giving up, he picked up the phone.

"Room service? Our window won't open." There was a chuckle at the other end as he continued, "Could you come up and have a look?"

Within minutes, a bellboy rapped on the door. He approached the tall window grinning from ear to ear, turned the latch, then slammed the flat of his palm into the bottom of the window. It reacted like a vertical seesaw. The top half of the window shifted six inches into their room. The bottom half now jutted six inches into the balcony.

"Good heavens!" was all he could say.

"It's to keep the monkeys out," he was informed. "When we had normal windows, the monkeys would enter through the opening. They stole food and anything brightly coloured. Once, they took off with a handbag. These latest windows were designed to keep them out." He smiled unctuously awaiting his tip. "And sir, please leave nothing on the balcony unattended, not even for a minute," the bell boy warned.

He shook his head in disbelief. "If they're such a nuisance, why not round them up and ship 'em out?"

The boy smirked, "Because legend has it that so long as the monkeys remain in Gibraltar, the British will too. If they go, who'll protect us from Spain?"

Finally, they were alone. He tentatively opened the balcony door and stepped out.

Once again, the sea view that he'd paid extra for wasn't exactly as touted. Yes, they were facing the sea. Although situated high on a hill, three-quarters of the view was obliterated by large, scrawny plane trees fanned out across the road. But at least he could smell the tang of brine and feel the breeze lapping against his cheeks. In between the trees, merchant ships laden three stories high with containers wended their way across the placid sun-splashed water into the Mediterranean.

As his family bustled in and out of their room—the boys had a suite of their own next door—he slumped back onto the bed and switched on the TV, not expecting much. Lo and behold! The English Premier League was on. It was the first match of the season. Leicester, his favourite team, was playing Arsenal at home. The game was about to start. Bliss. He raided a Fry's Turkish Delight chocolate bar from his cache of goodies, stole a can of Coke from the mini bar when

Laura wasn't looking and settled himself down to enjoy the rest of the afternoon.

No sooner had he done so, Laura cajoled him. "Come, let's unpack and go look around."

With a sigh, he acceded. Scoffing down his last bite of chocolate and quaffing down the remains of his Coke, he tumbled out of bed mumbling to himself, "No rest for the wicked."

The Rock Hotel balanced itself precariously on its perch halfway up a hill. The squat, sparkling-white structure sprawled across the hillside, reminding him of the white cliffs of Dover. As they entered the narrow road, there were no pedestrians in sight. It was siesta time. Who would be parading the streets in this hot afternoon weather anyway, except tourists? They stayed on the narrow path curving down Europa Road. Tall trees hovered over them from behind walled gardens ofancient stone houses. Here and there, narrow black iron gates broke the monotony. Pering through their grilles, he saw small, tile-covered, shaded courtyards leading to porticos within. Purple and crimson bougainvillea sprouted along wooden trestles. Large pots containing a plethora of chrysanthemums of burnished gold, sky-blue and pale lime green.

At the bottom of the hill, they passed through an arch—the gateway into the town.

Within minutes they were in front of Marks and Spencer.

"Wait here," he pointed to a bench. "I'll be right back."

He dashed in and jumped onto the escalator to the basement food department. When he got there, he gasped. The shelves were bare.

"What happened?" he asked the cashier.

In a tone of sheer hopelessness, she murmured, "Two cruise ships hit port at the same time. Their passengers bought the lot. If only you'd come an hour ago."

It seemed a plague of locusts had descended, leaving nought in their wake. The sight of empty shelves and endless line ups on an island of barely seven miles square repeated itself wherever they went.

They progressed towards the quaint town square where stores were even tinier than they had been in England and were filled with watches and jewellery at bargain prices. Limestone hills dominated the sleepy square, out of which the locals had carved caverns for artisan workshops. Gibraltar's great attraction lay in its tax-free status. Once a boon to the locals in attracting tourists beyond rowdy, well-oiled matelots, acting solely as a way station for the British Royal Navy, Gibraltar's tax-free status became a curse. As well as being the untrammelled domain of bargain-hungry tourists, Gibraltar was now the residence of the world's super rich.

From the town square a path led to a marina. Here, the island's centuries-old architecture was eschewed, replaced by towers of luxury condominiums and glittering glass facades of professional buildings housing lawyers and accountants required to quench the all-consuming thirsts of their billionaire clients. Unbeknownst, they had entered the glitz and glamour of Hollywood. Multi-million-dollar yachts, larger than their home in Canada, littered the marina. A steppingstone away, restaurants—just shy of a Michelin star—hid in the shade of alleyways, always open to the dictates of their patrons.

Their day of travel and walking through the sun-drenched afternoon left them exhausted.

"Hon, can we take a taxi home?" Laura pleaded. Her shoulders drooped under the weight of multi-coloured hand-blown glass goblets purchased to fill her china cabinet.

Just then, a red minibus, empty of passengers, came to a halt in front of them.

"Need a lift?" the driver enquired. Although his English idiom was flawless, the slight slur of accent acquired by years of living beside Spain, marked him as a native.

They climbed aboard and dropped into a seat with a sigh of relief. Ascending a hill soon after, he nudged Laura, "Look, there's the airport." It was built on reclaimed land to the north, bordering Spain, their age-old enemy. Traffic crossed the runway to get from Spain into Gibraltar and vice-versa. The road was barred by a wooden arm as it would have been at any ordinary railway crossing. An endless line of cars in both directions waited patiently for a plane to land as did dozens of pedestrians glancing nonchalantly as it whizzed past them only a few feet away.

Turning a corner, they could see the town on one side and, well below them on the other side, pristine sandy beaches with not a tourist in sight. Perhaps these were the last pockets of sanctuary of the island's browbeaten native population.

At the highest point, the bus came to a halt.

"We'll be here for twenty minutes," the driver announced. "Go visit our monkeys." You have enough time. I'll watch over your shopping."

With no hesitation they took up his offer, leaving all the treasures they had collected with a complete stranger.

A dozen monkeys congregated on an open oblong slab of concrete. They were surrounded by tourists. A baby monkey jumped onto the shoulder of an elderly lady clutching a walking stick. While she was distracted, hordes of sightseers recorded the action for posterity with their Leicas and iPhones. Seizing the opportunity, the rest of the monkeys scattered and raided the tourists in a well-coordinated smash-and-grab manoeuvre—a handbag, some colourfully loud jewellery and fruit were carried away, leaving their victims astonished and bewildered by their fate.

In total disarray, they turned to seek help. There was none. Meanwhile, the monkeys, perched atop rocks a hundred feet out of reach, fought over the spoils. Then, the monkey with the handbag returned, dumping the bag on the ground, staring at the owner as if inviting a ransom in exchange.

He couldn't help smiling at the monkey attempting to dictate terms. His heart went out to the mischief-maker in kindred sympathy. Decades ago, he too had stood his ground to gain control of his destiny.

Back in October 1973, on failing his high school exams he sought solace in a summer of travel against his mother's wishes. It had been her highest ambition to watch her son graduate from Oxford or Cambridge.

"The easiest way would be to have him take maths and science at high school," she had been told by her confidantes.

He abhorred the subjects and repeatedly failed his class work, assignments and finally his exams. For that, she chastised him for being an utter failure.

"Just like your dad," who also could never live up to her expectations, languishing his whole work life in some minor clerical position.

Until then, he had been trained since childhood to follow every instruction laid down by his mother. That path led him across one minefield to the next of broken ambitions and plummeting confidence. Having concentrated on his weaknesses all his life, what did she expect?

"I'm travelling first." He was putting his foot down.

His father, an airline employee, furnished him with free travel tickets. His first stop was Beirut, Lebanon. The money he had saved was a pittance. He had two options for accommodation—either sleeping on airport floors or befriending fellow passengers who would invite him to stay with them for a few days and show him around. This time, he wasn't so lucky and resigned himself to sleeping at the airport. He landed in the evening and searched for a corner to lie down in. Suddenly, he heard the screaming whine of nose-diving aircraft, then thundering explosions followed by a staccato of gunfire.

A soldier found him huddled, covering his ears. "You can't stay here. The airport is under attack," he blurted, nudging him with his rifle.

"I have no money. It's nighttime. Can I stay until the morning?" And the nightmare began.

This was the start of the Yom Kippur War. The Egyptians, led by President Sadat, launched a sneak attack on the Israelis on their holiest of days. The war spilled into Lebanon, Syria and other neighbouring countries. The airport was closed indefinitely. Now he had to find a way overland to Teheran, Iran to catch his ongoing flights. The only exit was a circuitous route by taxi (which he shared with four other passengers and a colicky baby) to Damascus over the Golan Heights, then local buses to the Gulf coast of Iraq and into Iran through its port of Abadan. Another bus ride north to Teheran would finally secure his safety.

He managed it. Through his eighteen-year-old eyes, each day was an adventure. To others, it might seem a nightmare. But he was FREE to own his destiny—good or bad. By luck or gall he survived. It engrained in him a sense of independence and, for once, restored confidence in himself. But now onward, all normal life would be tough to bear.

Out of the frying pan into... a pool of glue. On his return to England, his mother found him a place at a nearby firm of Chartered Accountants. He stared back at her coldly. She waved his letter of invitation in front of him in celebration. At least, if he couldn't go to university, he would end up in a respected career that she could trumpet to her afternoon tea coterie.

"Think about it," she harangued. "In five years, you'll have the world at your feet at such a young age, while your university friends will still be looking for a job." She wasn't finished. "You should thank Sam when you see him."

Sam was a close family friend—the only one who supported him in his tribulations on failing his exams. It was Sam who persuaded Mum to allow him into accounting, rather than have him repeat his last year at school. Sam had recently qualified and been promoted to manager at his firm. Once again, his life had been shanghaied for the next five years.

On a cold, damp, miserable grey January morning he entered the portal of Hale and Company with the demeanour of a prisoner resigned to serve his full sentence.

Hale and Co. spelt 'Doomsville' for him. The firm operated out of an old Victorian house. Typical of that bygone era, he was escorted to the attic, where servants would have been quartered, to join several other articled clerks in training. A dormer window let in the only light, as colourless as his fellow inmates—such a contrast from the blazing sunlight he had left behind on his travels. He stared at his damp paper bag of sandwiches, longing for his erstwhile daily meal of Manaish, a pizza of unleavened dough brushed with olive oil and sprinkled with sumac, a lemony-tasting herb—the local poor man's diet.

Overnight he had been shoved into a straitjacket of regimented, sedentary time, overburdened with a tedious, repetitive workload. He arrived at nine, lunch was at one, and the office closed at five. Each day Mr. Griffiths, his managing partner, came and delivered him a suitcase, large carrier bag, or box of invoices and bank statements from the local butcher or mechanic. He tabulated the information and returned it to the partner at day's end. Every ounce of initiative or flair that he had discovered in himself during his travels were an anathema to his colleagues and employers. Was this to be his sentence for the next five years? He shuddered at the thought, completely heartbroken.

A year passed. He had learned nothing more than bookkeeping. There was no progression to preparing financial statements or tax returns. These were all handled by Mr. Griffiths whenever he had the inclination. Meanwhile, he sat for his first set of exams and, once again, failed miserably, much to his mother's chagrin but, more painfully, the sad disappointment of Sam, who had tried so hard to sustain him.

To hell with it all. Why not quit to find something he really liked to do? A past conversation with Sam rose in his memory.

"Once you're qualified, you have an open ticket to travel and work anywhere in the world," he had said. That was the carrot.

Additionally, he didn't want to leave the firm branded as a failure and affirm his mother's contention. If he left the profession, all the past misery he had suffered would have been in vain. He would probably be forced to retake his school exams—another year wasted. Why not spend a few years more to acquire his designation? He thought about it constantly, always returning to the conclusion that a larger, more modern firm was the only answer to his problem. It was time to consult Sam.

His frustrated mentor sat behind his desk, twiddling a pencil between his fingers as he heard him out.

"They won't allow you to transfer. It would be a major embarrassment to them. No one changes firms in the middle of their articleship. If you hand in your notice, no other accounting firm will hire you for fear of offending our firm. Stick it out with us. Once you qualify, you can go on your way—as far away as possible from your mother I expect."

Fine advice. But to his way of thinking, prolonging his stay here would spell disaster, the same if he quit. He had to persuade the firm to let him transfer.

The obvious strategy was to make constant errors in his work.

"The boy's lost his marbles," became the common cry. But instead of agreeing to a transfer, they changed his work. Joan, their receptionist, was due for maternity leave. He was given the run of the front office.

For a month he fumed in silence, seeing no advance in achieving his goal. It was time to ramp up the pressure on the partners, to gain their attention again.

Hale and Co. operated three bank accounts for themselves and their clients. Alongside his responsibility as receptionist, he was tasked to visit each bank to make deposits. The following Tuesday he began his new assignment. By the time he got to the second bank, it had a long line up. He decided to take his lunch break first and entered Wimpy's, the burger joint. Finishing his lunch, he discarded his wrapper. A thought struck him. Surreptitiously, confirming no one was watching, he bent down, grabbed the bank book, and tossed it into the garbage bin.

Later that day, an impromptu meeting was held by the partners. He overheard them in the boardroom on his way out that evening.

"What's the world coming to?" roared Mr. Hale, the senior partner. "Now every Tom, Dick and Harry will know our business if they find that deposit book."

The outcome? Next day, instead of a pink slip of dismissal, he was handed a slim, black attaché case. It contained three bank deposit books safely locked inside. To his utmost frustration, they still had not thrown in the towel. What more could he do?

The temptation was too great. On his very next outing, he lost the hallowed case.

"Dunno what happened," was all he could think of as an excuse.

"Must've left it at the bus stop."

At his interrogation, the senior partner was beside himself. "Why did you catch a bus? I thought you always walked."

"It was raining cats and dogs. I forgot me raincoat. Didn't want to get me suit wet." He glared back at his employer.

They relegated his tasks to only answering the phone. Mr. Murcott, the junior partner, was given the banking duty. His shenanigans hadn't helped one bit.

The following week, as he manned reception, he heard the gerontic Mr. Hale coughing and spluttering like an old steam engine as he pounded down the stairs, appearing to miss a step, by the sound of it. The whole town of Maidenhead must have heard him curse. What was the old codger trying to do? Practise a complex ballet movement? The founding partner almost broke the reception door down. In his haste, he had forgotten to turn the handle.

"You...you..." he kept repeating. "What are those workmen doing in our parking lot?"

"They're delivering stuff. Building materials, I think. Why? Something wrong?" he asked innocently.

Of course, something was wrong. He had created it purposely. As part of their service, the firm acted as the registered office of their clients. All invoices had both of the addresses on them—the registered office address as well its actual business address. The workmen had arrived brandishing a delivery note displaying both addresses. It took a minute to direct them to the back of the house instead of to the business address.

Mr. Hale swallowed what air he could press into his collapsing lungs. "They're not for us you imbecile. They're for a client. They got the wrong address."

With that, the chief charged headlong out of the room and hurtled down the stairs leading to the parking lot. He followed suit, not wanting to miss one bit of the action.

The once lovely long garden of Hale House had long since been paved over to accommodate the partners' and clients' cars.

As Mr. Hale entered the fray, the workers were finishing their unloading. Stacks upon stacks of corrugated iron sheets now formed an impregnable wall several feet high, blocking the exit way.

"Take them back immediately," the chief bellowed.

They stared back at him in total disbelief. Their foreman spoke up. "Sorry mate, do you understand how long it took us to unload this lot? Now you want us to cart them back. Didn't your receptionist confirm this was the address?"

Later that afternoon, he overheard Mr. Hale on the phone bawling out his junior partner, responsible for hiring him on Sam's advice. "Enough of his monkey business. You have to arrange his transfer immediately. God knows what the young devil will do next. Probably burn the house down."

His reverie was shattered by the shriek of his boys and the tugging of his T-shirt.

"Pop, look!" The boys howled with laughter. "See what the monkey did with the handbag?"

For a couple of apples and a bunch of grapes, the monkey had capitulated, leaving the handbag in his wake as he retreated, with his hands full of booty, back to his community atop the rocks. The crowd of tourists dispersed quickly and quietly, clutching their goods and valuables tightly to them, constantly peering over their shoulder on the lookout for further attacks. There were none.

He heard a honk. The bus driver was waving them back. They sat down, their laps overladen with goblets, gifts, and gimcracks.

As the sun gradually set over the blue-green glittering ocean, Alex leaned forward, "Pops, where are you taking us tomorrow?"

"Wait and see," he answered, sporting a wicked smile.

AUTHOR'S NOTE

O! Those monkeys. Those monkeys.
How I empathized with their desire to be the masters
of their universe.

ILLUSTRATOR'S NOTE

Surviving being in a situation that you didn't want to be
in the first place can take some real creative effort—even
becoming a saboteur in the eyes of your 'betters'. Those
monkeys are just making an advantageous reality out of
a situation they found themselves thrust into!

CHAPTER 5

ROCK BOTTOM

"WHERE'S OUR GUIDE?" he asked anxiously, examining his watch again. The man was an hour late.

The same concierge who had booked the tour of Gibraltar for his family yesterday grimaced. "Sir, another cruise ship entered port early this morning. Everything is delayed," he remarked peevishly. "Most drivers and guides are still dealing with incoming passengers. Let me call their office."

He searched for his family and found them seated at a nearby coffee table. Laura was absorbed in her slim guidebook on Gibraltar while the boys were engrossed in a game of gin rummy for points—no signs of impatience or sympathy.

There was a harried conversation between the concierge and the person on the other end of the phone. The concierge hung up the phone. "He'll be here within the hour."

He shook his head in dismay. This was their only full day here.

He had booked a private tour as a surprise for his family. Now it seemed they were happier sitting and playing cards.

Over an hour later, a man, as thin as a rasher of bacon, doffing a royal blue cap with a scarlet band around it, made his way meekly toward them. He apologized abjectly. "Terribly sorry for the delay. My manager double-booked me. Would you mind sharing me with a couple from New Jersey?" he pleaded sheepishly. "They're on their honeymoon."

What could he say? He gestured to Laura, hoping she'd complain. All he heard from her was "On honeymoon? How lovely."

He smiled at her through gritted teeth, raising his head and palms to the rococo ceiling when no one was looking.

The newly-weds turned out to be in their sixties, both vying to top three hundred pounds. Their attire marked them as Hasidic Jews. The husband wore a large, ink-black, brimmed fedora. A thick grey-white beard covered his face, while long curls trailed down from the sides of his hat. His beloved was plastered in a long grey dress. A simple long-sleeved white blouse covered her neckline. The blouse was overhung with a dark, plain shawl. An equally plain black scarf hid her hair. They spoke not a word, placing themselves compactly in the two rear seats. The front seats were left to his family.

He climbed into the van and found himself clutching the steering wheel.

"Sir, you're in my seat. Remember, here we drive on the left," the milksop smiled sardonically. "By the way, my name's Steve," as though his introduction helped in any way.

There was a judder as Steve shifted the gear manually. With a hop and a jump, the van shoved off.

He gulped down a swig of water from his bottle and prayed.

Flamenco music caterwauled from the radio, drowning every syllable Steve imparted. Behind the wheel, his tepid personality erupted as though he had taken a restorative. He executed a daredevil U-turn in the narrowest of streets in front of the hotel, making his passenger question the adequacy of his travel insurance. The engine lurched itself up the hill.

It seemed no sooner had they started, they abruptly braked, as though the van had given up the ghost. Steve had parked in a lay-by, minutes from their hotel, The Rock. He shook his head in disbelief. They could have walked over.

A large placard in white, yellow, and blue welcomed them to St. Michael's Cave. Through a crack in the rock, the maw of a humungous cavern greeted them. It wasn't the beautifully coloured rocks pulsating under revolving spotlights that took his breath away, but rows upon rows of seats—perhaps a hundred—all tiered up a slope, as if in a cinema or auditorium. The aisle between the adjacent rows led down to the stage where strobe lights highlighted more crystalline rocks of spectacular rainbow colours. Giant speakers boomed out *Another One Bites the Dust* by the rock band Queen. The pitch was perfect, the reverberation deafening.

The boys were, as usual, well ahead of them, but for a change, Laura and he were not the last ones in the group. Plodding behind them, came the Hasidic newlyweds.

Steve led them behind the stage and directed them to a foot-wide path into the darker recesses of the cavern that ran into further, ever-smaller caves. "I'll meet you back at the entrance in half-an-hour." With that he disappeared.

They continued into the claustrophobic void. The all-consuming darkness, and the sporadic droplets of heavy water dripping down upon them transported him to a fogbound winter afternoon in England, marooned in an attic office, training as an accountant.

Only a shadow of light penetrated the solitary dormer window. Once again, the heat and electricity had been cut off. It was the 'Winter of Discontent' under Margaret Thatcher's regime. In retaliation to her mandate to reduce the power of the unions, they had resorted to carrying out revolving strikes resulting in recurrent outages. Miserably dank afternoons were spent waiting in frustration for the lights to flicker on and heat to be restored.

He had started his articleship in January, returning from a six-month sojourn in the Middle East, a blazing sun-blanched land riven by constant war, the latest of which he had walked into by happenstance—the surprise Egyptian attack dubbed the Yom Kippur War. Armed with that experience, his companions at the large oaken table, set plumb in the middle of the attic, seemed as insipid as the enervating climate. His fellow clerks responded in kind. No one was interested in his past travels. None cared for his sardonic remarks. No one befriended him. As his enthusiasm flagged, so did his level of work—an added burden to be suffered by his colleagues. He failed his exams. Moving inexorably towards termination, he lived in suspended animation, waiting to be fired or his articleship ended. He headed into a glacial, inexorable decline toward a dead end of helplessness and despair.

Cooped up in St. Michael's Cave they realized they were lost. There was no sight of the route they had taken to get here.

Laura tapped his shoulder. "Hon, which way do we go now?" The newly-weds had disappeared too. After several failed attempts, they finally found the exit, gathering momentum with each step. They were minutes away from their rendezvous with Steve when they collided unceremoniously into their travelling companions.

Their guide was at the entrance, fidgeting with his keys. "Your boys are in the van waiting for you. Follow me."

Steve drove them to the top of the hill, then veered sharply down the other side.

He closed his eyes a lot of the way, fearing a crash into the oncoming traffic. There was never any room for two cars to pass each other. Lay-bys showed up every half mile with one or the other vehicle steering into them, to let the other go past. Oddly, there was no blaring of horns as in other countries. Drivers seemed to know instinctively when to stop or carry on.

The next excursion was to a warren of tunnels dug deep into the limestone hills. In one of the interminable wars fought with Spain from the time the Royal Navy had captured Gibraltar, a Royal Engineer had devised this defence system of outposts facing Spain.

Through these tunnels, seamen had rolled their ships' cannons to these vantage points to bombard the Spanish invaders. Tiny rooms had been carved all along the tunnels. Today, they were populated with life-sized wax models of soldiers sleeping, eating, or manning their gunnery. They were still inspected daily, not by their commanders, but by an endless row of tourists.

A heavy oak door barred their entrance. Through a square hole with vertical iron bars, he observed a Spanish prisoner lying asleep on the wet limestone floor. He himself knew what it was like to be a prisoner.

So desperate was he at his own plight at Hale & Co., that he ventured to do the unthinkable. He sought his mother's advice.

For decades, the two had had running skirmishes and full-fledged battles. His mother always knew what was best for him—at least she thought she did. Her Herculean personality left no room to argue but was instead a smouldering fuse to a barrel of gunpowder about to explode. She had insisted he take science at school to further her attempts to gain him entrance to Cambridge. He loved history and geography, but found science incomprehensible. He failed almost every test and assignment, including his high school exams, when so much more was expected of him. Demoralized, he did little to resist her call to become a Chartered Accountant, a respected, if not revered member of society. That decision sank him further into a quagmire of defeat and despondency, from which he ironically sought solace from his mother.

"Mum, what can I do to cope with all this? I can't sleep at night, I'm so anxious. I can't seem to get anything right. Perhaps a psychiatrist could help. What do you think?"

Her eyes drilled into him, betraying her annoyance at being disturbed while watching her role model, Margaret Thatcher, on TV.

"My son going to see a psycho? You must be mad!"

There was a pause in their proceedings until the next commercial break.

"Here's where you go." She tore off a sheet of lavender-blue note- paper, inscribed with her personal initials from a pad on her side table, retrieved her Queen's Silver Jubilee fountain pen from beneath her Times of London newspaper and, like her heroine, prescribed her cure. Task accomplished, she raised her hand to command silence. Her show had restarted.

He read and reread her note in utter bewilderment. It was an address in Golders Green, a suburb of London, where the many of the most affluent Jews lived. Who did she know there? She was an East Indian Muslim out of Africa for God's sake.

"I'll make you an appointment tomorrow. Now leave me in peace," was all he could wheedle out of her. The bloody programme had begun again.

In the tunnel, a distinct cough brought him back to his senses. The line of sightseers behind him were growing impatient. He turned to his wife and accompanied her to the exit into the waiting arms of Steve and the rest of his party.

The van started. He was lulled into a false sense of security until he was jarred to the bone—Steve had run over a pothole. They continued lurching downhill toward the southernmost tip of Gibraltar. After a while, he continued his reverie.

The whole trip to Golders Green was a mixture of hope and trepidation.

Mum had been as good as her word. He was to present himself the following Saturday at 10 a.m. How was he to get there so early in the morning? Maidenhead, where he lived, was a forty-minute ride to Paddington, London. Golders Green was another two changes on the Underground. All he was given was an address. He still had to find the place. His mum gave neither the name of the person or the business. He was to go through the side gate of a house and knock at the back door.

With the help of passersby, he arrived in the nick of time. Catching his breath, he knocked.

A husky female Russian voice bade him enter. The door opened at his touch. Behind a large walnut-veneered desk sat an elderly lady with bright golden-red hair, heavily made up. Her bosom was large, heaving under her tight clothing. A flimsy light grey silk blouse complemented a garish leopard-skin leotard. On the wall behind her were framed blown-up photographs in the style purveyed in socialite magazines, of a short, thin, dapper man, always in a grey pin-striped suit and tie in the company of film stars, politicians, and other celebrities.

She stood up, towering over his five-foot-four-inch frame and clenched his hand in a wrestler's grip. "Follow me," she commanded.

Leading him down a corridor, she stopped at a door at the end. She knocked before ushering him in. After accomplishing her duty, she evacuated the room immediately, closing the door behind her.

In his dark, heavily curtained sanctuary, sat the man in the photos. His standard grey suit hung shapelessly on his emaciated body. With no other lighting, a desk lamp shone to one side of his face leaving a chiaroscuro—one half of his visage in glaring white light and the other in portentous darkness. The man rose. He was barely five foot tall. He appeared to be distinctly Pakistani. What was he doing in Golders Green?

Instead of shaking his hand and introducing himself, the man ordered him to sit down opposite him and hold out his palms on the table. The next minute, the man took out a paint roller and tray from his side drawer. The tray appeared to hold black paint. The man dipped the roller in, then plastered the paint all over his client's palms. He then grabbed the painted palms, turned them over and planted them firmly onto a large piece of tracing paper.

The man then burst into a frenzy of activity. Opening a tin of geometry instruments, he began to draw lines across the imprints of his client's palms.

Breaking his solemn silence, the man bombarded him with rapid-fire questions. "What is the date of your birth?" he rasped. "Where and at what time?" all the while measuring and remeasuring the lines drawn on paper. Once done, he grabbed his client's hands and scrutinized them under his lamp. A large round silver-handled magnifying glass was used to compare the paper prints to his actual palms to ensure none of the fine lines were missed.

"You've seen much of this world. Seen much turmoil," he whispered in a voice from an ancient souk, weak and wavering. "You are deeply unhappy with your life and work," he continued. "You will encounter years more of unhappiness in both. A tumult of changes. Of beginnings and turbulent endings. A flight across water to a desolate land far, far away. This is not a time to waver but to endure and survive. An opportunity will come to escape... eventually... Years of unhappiness and strife will come before you find peace."

At the end, the man, still not proffering his name, asked, "Any questions?"

Stunned, his head feeling as though pounded by a sledgehammer, he could utter no words. Should he ask for a refund? Then again, he wasn't asked to pay. How had Mum wangled this? Thinking of her, he wanted to scream. How could she do this to him, sundering any hope he had left? For the love of him, the man's words kept throbbing in his brain. "Unhappiness and discontent. A journey to the middle of nowhere—an exile?"

Thanking the man, glad to be rid of him, he walked out cursing his mother all the way to the station. *"Only time will tell."* What would it tell?

The shaking, rattling minivan came to a halt in the open parking lot of Europa Point.

A lighthouse afforded a view across Algeciras Bay and the African coast on the other side. A quintessentially English cricket ground stuck out at one end, a newly erected mosque—funded by Saudi Arabia—at the other.

The sunshiny weather was perfect—not too hot. It was complemented by the fresh breeze from the sea. The sight of Africa drew him to his birthplace, the Union Jack raised high on a flagpole, to his struggles in England.

Atop the lighthouse, he watched his family running off to take photos of a memorial to fallen soldiers. He stared out across the glittering water, his fortune as endless as the sea.

AUTHOR'S NOTE

*How could a mother, observing the desperation in her son,
exhort him to visit a chiromancer?*

*What incensed me more was the man himself.
You always wish the fortune told you comes true.
It was the most dismal prediction. And it all came true.
I'm NEVER tempted to go back to him, lest
I throw a brick at him.*

ILLUSTRATOR'S NOTE

*Escaping the expected! Weird or even scary situations and
(even weirder) characters become personal building blocks
in slightly skewed, but colourful, origin stories and the
ways you escaped other's unwanted predictions
and plans for you.*

"A glorious sight awaited him…"

CHAPTER 6

CATHEDRAL IN THE DARK

THE SMALL WHITE stuccoed bungalow could have been transplanted from the very English council estate where he was brought up, but there was no mistaking the two. Behind the bungalow loomed the Rock of Gibraltar, rising through the mist like a colossus, blotting out the hazy early morning sunshine. The building was no humble dwelling but, according to their taxi driver, was the border checkpoint into Spain.

There was no activity. Not a soul in sight. The entrance door was shut. He knocked and waited. No answer. He knocked again.

He waved his hands at his family in frustration. He had woken them up at the ungodly hour of 5:30 a.m. to get here, anticipating a long queue and the Spanish red tape delaying them further in catching their 8 a.m. train from Algeciras to Seville. He remonstrated with their taxi driver. "We asked you to take us to the station, not dump us here in the middle of nowhere."

"Sir, taxis from Gibraltar cannot cross the border. You have to clear customs, then find a Spanish taxi on the other side." With that the driver about-turned, leaving them with their mouths hanging open.

Laura stood beside him with her arms folded. "Now what do we do?" The boys sat dejectedly on their suitcases gazing up at their father for guidance.

He knocked once again. The door creaked open. He looked surreptitiously from left to right then entered.

"You can't do that!" Laura almost screamed." That's trespassing. They could ban us for life."

He glanced at his watch. It was 7:15 a.m. It would take forty-five minutes to get to the station. If they missed their connection, they would be stranded in some provincial town overnight. The whole itinerary would go up in smoke, including the prepaid five-star hotel that cost a bomb. He had no choice. He darted in.

The place was deserted. It was one long room divided in half by a tall counter, behind which stood the exit door. He beckoned his family in silence with his finger. Poor Laura glanced hither and thither, running as fast as she could through the building. Smiles broke out on his boys' faces to watch Pops breaking rules he had hammered into them to follow since they were toddlers. The eerie silence was broken by the trundling of their luggage.

Outside the door, a large billboard greeted them. Welcome to Spain. Below it, a row of tiny taxis held their ground, like snorting baby bulls draped in saffron orange and yellow, while their drivers perused newspapers, had a smoke or snoozed. He chose the nearest car and spoke up in his best upper-class English. "The railway station, please. And hurry," automatically assuming the driver understood him.

The road to the station followed the grey, tossing sea to one side and tall seedy apartment buildings on the other. Their once-white coating had greyed and their paint was peeling off everywhere. Tiny balconies indicated how small each unit was. Algeciras served as a bedroom community to Gibraltar, where the cost of housing was prohibitive. Scrawny, brown-grassed open squares distanced the buildings from the road. Here and there, dogs, as thin as rakes, ran unleashed, their stout, elderly owners puffing to catch up. Sheets of newspaper danced in the wind. They caught on lampposts, only to be set free again by the fickle sea wind.

They hit the motorway for a while then re-entered the town. Dirt-ridden, dishevelled streets were stained with graffiti. The station was as old and decrepit as the rest of the town they had passed through. No sign that prosperity had ever existed here. He wondered if the rest of their journey would be the same—a catalogue of poverty and misery.

A gatekeeper pointed out their train—it was the only one in the station. As they installed themselves comfortably in their seats, the train shunted its way out. Its rhythm lulled his family to sleep, leaving him to ponder on an earlier journey he had embarked on to a new job in England.

He had spent two years training as an accountant. It was hopeless. His standard of work was awful and he continually failed his exams. It was no surprise then to be called to report to Sam, the office manager. Expecting to receive his walking papers, he was flabbergasted to witness the man smiling.

Hale & Co. had found a firm he could transfer to. It was in Slough, a neighbouring town. Sam had arranged an appointment the next day with Huw Griffiths, the senior partner there.

The train to his interview passed Taplow, where his mother had stayed in a converted manor house renting a flat for several years. Eric, his best friend, lived near the next stop at Dorney Reach. Burnham Grammar School, which he had recently attended was located in a village—the penultimate stop from Slough.

His interview with Mr. Griffiths lasted barely half-an-hour. He was a roly-poly man, young for his position, probably in his thirties, but as bald as a coot, save for one lock of hair fighting gallantly to retain a foothold. Unlike the punctilious manner and dress practised by his current employer, the man wore a suit crumpled to such a degree that it looked as though it had been slept in. His garish red tie was skewed to one side, seemingly glued to a badly scuffed, yellowing white dress shirt. The man smiled. "Call me Huw." Quite a change from the obligatory "Mr." used without question where he currently worked. "Our staff are either Chartered Accountants or highly experienced. We don't believe in articled clerks. They're an expensive luxury." With no further explanation, Huw veered off onto another topic. "Can you drive? We have a Mini Cooper you can use. You'll be travelling all over the country on audits."

No wonder Sam had chosen this firm for him. He'd travelled independently all his life then found himself cooped up in an attic of an office performing one monotonous task after another—deskbound. He smiled enthusiastically. "No. But I'm taking a test next week." He didn't mention his mother was forcing him to or that he had already failed his test several times, continuously taking lessons for the past two years. Now, he was motivated.

"Good. One of my staff left. We need a replacement right away. Can you start next week? Sam tells me you're in your third year. That should be enough experience for you to join us."

Without giving him a chance to speak, Huw proceeded. "We'll start you off at five thousand a year, four weeks paid study leave and another two weeks paid holiday. You'll have to work independently. No one's got the time to train you."

He could have hugged the man. His salary today was six hundred pounds a year with a measly two week unpaid study leave. It was like winning the lottery ticket. He accepted at once.

"Come in next Monday. I won't be around, but one of the boys will show you the ropes."

It wasn't until he was outside and slapped in the face by a wintry gust, that he came to his senses. What had he let himself in for? Till now, all he had learned was elementary bookkeeping, let alone preparing or auditing financial statements. How long was he going to last?

The Spanish train rumbled on. Laura slept in fits and starts, the boys fully unconscious all the way. He stared out the window, blasting the railway system to himself. All lines led to Madrid, in the centre of Spain, like a spider's web. To reach Seville, which was in the south, they had to catch the Madrid train going north, get off at Córdoba, then change to a southern train to Seville. It doubled the travelling time, never mind an extra hour wait in Córdoba.

Its station came as a surprise. Córdoba was a provincial town, having the dubious honour of being the capital of Islamic Spain way back in 756 CE when Muslims ruled half of Spain for four hundred years. To him, it was a backwater to be visited for its historical Mezquita-Catedral. He expected to enter a semi-derelict station, similar to the one in Algeciras. That definitely wasn't the case. The edifice was a recently minted glass palace to rival any major station in Europe. On disembarking, they were carried up sparkling escalators from the trains below, to the main, high-roofed concourse. A large border of glass separated its walls from the roof to let in an inordinate mass of sunlight.

The concourse was packed. Restaurants vied with shops for space on both sides of a wide corridor. At the centre of the long thorough-fare were a throng of plastic seats fixed to a skeleton frame of blue steel. All seats were occupied by passengers and their luggage. Their tags haled them from every part of the world. Local men in smart light-grey suits, mothers with their infants buckled in their strollers intermingled with students in gashed blue jeans and Jesus boots. A buzz of energy activated the scene.

Alex and Chris saw a McDonald's at one end of the station. They dragged their mother with them. "Leave your bags with me. I'll find a seat. Come look for me when you're done," he instructed.

He settled beside two female students from Philadelphia. "We got a week off, bought a couple of cheap air tickets, a Europass and here we are on a day trip."

He compared the three days his family would spend here next week. Beyond taking pictures in front of monuments, how could they appreciate or understand this vast country and its inhabitants?

His family always spent at least a month on each trip to gain a true experience of a land and its people. Perhaps they were lucky to be so privileged. Perhaps it was better to experience a week than nothing at all.

Around him he noticed two currents of passersby. Tourists swarmed McDonald's, locals a large cafeteria. When his brood returned and took charge of his burden, he joined the locals. Observing someone eating a thick, triangular slice of omelette, he pointed it out to the server. "Tortilla De Patatas"—potato omelette with green peppers and onions the way his grandmother would make. He added bags of crisps and bars of fruit nougat to his tally.

Departure time arrived. For a little extra, they sat in first class facing each other across a wide table. The journey to Seville would take another hour and a half. They might as well take advantage of the upgrade, which included light refreshments and drinks.

Their energy restored, Chris unrolled a chess board and challenged his brother to a game.

"Hon, where are we staying in Seville?"

"The Catedral Hotel, right in the heart of medieval old town. It'll be one of the best we stay at."

"Really?"

"You know I always choose one-of-a-kind hotels for us? Well, this one's converted out of a row of fourteen medieval houses facing the cathedral. They left the exterior as is, then constructed forty rooms within them. The Catedral has been rated the best boutique hotel in Seville." He pointed to her iPad. "Go look it up. They were booked solid. Thank goodness for a last-minute cancellation."

"You're right. It's so pretty." She showed him the exterior— a glittering white stucco building, three storeys high with tiny quaint balconies, their intricate filigree cast iron railings in shiny black.

"And knowing these boutique hotels with their small number of rooms, the service should be very personal."

Alex overheard and chimed in. "Does that mean we'll be in the centre of all the action?"

"Yes. Imagine you'll be part of living history. I'm sure the rooms will reflect it too."

With that, the boys continued their game and Laura attended to her emails. He was once again left alone to his own thoughts and memories of his first day at Griffiths, Miles & Sully in Slough.

At Hale & Co. where he'd started his accounting, punctuality was drilled into him. Consequently, he arrived at his new office shortly before 9 a.m. Instead of a converted Victorian house, he was in-stalled in the second floor of a modern office block at the bottom of the high street. The glass door opened at his touch. He "Halloed." No answer. A narrow corridor led to the partners' offices. To the left was an open area partitioned by grey cloth screens, six feet tall. He poked his head around them. A typewriter confirmed it was the secretarial pool. To the right, a door opened to a large room with several desks facing each other. Oversized windows overlooked a parking lot at the back of the building. A high-rise commercial tower on the opposite end of the lot blocked all other views.

No one was in. He found the kitchen and made himself some tea.

His trepidation alternated with boredom and disappointment. The day's Daily Telegraph lay on the floor where the paperboy had chucked it. Having nothing else to do, he attacked the cross-word. By 9.30 a.m., the puzzle conquered, the news and sports sections perused, he had no idea what to do. The door opened. The first of the "boys" came through. "Oo are you mate?" the man questioned suspiciously.

He didn't know what to say. Surely, they knew he was arriving, didn't they? Without waiting for a reply, the man disappeared through the door. A few minutes later, he heard the kettle whistling in the kitchen. Two more of the team showed up and examined him for a moment. They too disappeared. Some more minutes passed. He could hear voices talking to each other but couldn't make out the conversation.

They all came back together. "Are you the new recruit?" the first one asked, "I'm Paul, the office manager. This is Ian." He nodded his head at a scrawny five-footer, so young looking he seemed to have graduated from high school yesterday.

"I'm Dennis." The third of the band was six-foot and broadshould -ered. With that they completely ignored him, all the while disc- ussing between them the latest football results and the squash game they played last night.

It was almost eleven before Paul came round to "Alright boys, time we started."

Expecting to be directed someway, watching them open files, he saw Paul stretch out for the Telegraph. "Now, let's put the crossword to bed." As he opened the page, there was a halt to his patter. The others waited for him, presumably to call out the clues. "Bloody 'ell! Oo's gawn an' dun the puzzle?" Paul cast an accusatory frown at the recruit. "Ev'ry morning for twenty years we bin havin' a go first fing in the morning. Now you've dun it," he glared at the rookie again." You've ruined ev'ryfing."

No one spoke to him again. They took to their desks with a sniff, leaving him with the only clear desk available.

The bullet train to Seville rocketed toward its destination. It was travelling so fast it gave him a headache just peeking out the window. He felt an elbow dig into him. Chris smiled unctuously at him—always a sign of danger.

"Pops, can you play chess with me? Alex is so boring." Mr. Charm personified. There it was, The Monster—an apt nom de guerre he had given his son—was once again after his money.

Pops was always an easy mark. It was far easier to beat him than his brother. The kid was obviously piling up his cash reserve for his trip. They played the best of five games. If either won three games in a row, in addition to a dollar, he would earn a bonus of five extra dollars. If abroad, they would use local currency. In the past, The Monster had been known to stall when approaching a different country whose currency value was higher.

The train blazed across its rails, sounding off like a ball-bearing running through a hollow tube. The scenery outside was pleasant as long as it remained open countryside speckled here and there with a lonely farmhouse. But it ruined your eyes if you tried to focus on one object, making you quite seasick. Before they could start, the rumbling of the refreshments cart along the aisle came to his rescue. "Later Chris, food's coming," he answered as charmingly as his son.

He lost his standard six euros—half as much again as his Canadian dollar—then reverted to playing Mastermind with Alex. By that time, they were heading into the suburbs of Seville.

Normally European train stations situated themselves in the centre of town, saving large amounts of taxi fares, rather than say, arriving from the airport. It was different here. The taxi took more than twenty minutes to reach The Catedral.

From sparkling sunshine, they were ushered into a dark cavern. All was black, except the all-white uniforms of the callow staff. The Catedral had wrung all the colour and passion out of the Spain of his dreams. They were asked to sit at what appeared to be frail Ikea sofas with thin black frames and black serge seats. Several assistants—students from across Europe speaking a plethora of languages, seconded here for the summer—asked for their passports, bombarding them with inexhaustible questions about where they had come from. All he wanted was an understanding host and a bed to lie in. The attendants had a list of questions to ask before then.

"Can we offer you a breakfast package? A dining package? A tour of an orangery? Seville is famous for its orange marmalade!"

He wanted to hire a guide for a private tour but thought the better of it. The attendants each meant well. It was their obligatory questionnaire he resented. It took almost an hour before they were released. Throughout the ordeal he held his ground, resolutely declining all their discounted offers. Was this hotel really given a five-star rating?

They fought a rearguard action towards the elevators. It was almost too small to fit them all in with their luggage. Finally, they made the second floor. At least they had adjacent rooms facing the cathedral, as promised when they booked. The boys scampered to their room abandoning them. He unlocked the door. Pitch darkness.

"Where's the light switch?" He could feel no bank of knobs on either side of the entrance. Laura found the bedside lamps and put them on. He wandered around the room in a daze. Everything was black, the entry room so claustrophobically small. Before they could reach the open room that housed their queen-sized bed, they had to negotiate the bathroom. Both sides of the narrow facility were glassed. Whosoever came into their room, could observe you naked if you took a shower, let alone the tiny toilet sequestered in one corner. All the walls were black. All the lighting, feeble in brightness, came from one source—the bedside tables. No overhead lighting. The windows were shuttered off in deep black wood—understandable as the afternoon temperature was its normal seasonal high of 45°C. He lowered himself into the only seat he could find, another vintage 1960s Ikea leftover—a black wire mesh seat, barely six inches off the ground in a flattened V-shape with a wafer of black cloth pillow to prevent the mesh permanently imprinting his bum. For a moment, he sat, shattered, scared to death that his chair would collapse under his weight and leave him with an unimaginable repair bill to pay.

He glimpsed his wife through the corner of one eye, waiting for her to complain. There was none of it.

"Oh! It's so cool in here" she chirruped, referring to the room temperature. "Get a hold of all the homemade soap, the perfume and oil-rich shampoo and conditioner in the bathroom. They have slippers for us to take home. And even bathrobes we can take to the pool."

The boys were no more help. They loved watching movies on their laptops in the dark without their parents complaining of eye strain. They rushed downstairs to the lobby to the ice cream parlour to purchase out-of-this-world locally made gelato. He was left alone to cavil.

What did he remember of the rest of the day? A long siesta to escape the sun; a walk in the evening to the nearest restaurant—not trusting The Catedral—and the downing of various tapas of squid, stuffed green peppers and ceviche.

In the middle of the night, he was awoken by the pop of an exhaust pipe and the whirr of a lonely motorbike. Laura remained undisturbed. Unable to sleep, he got up and opened the shutter to their balcony. A glorious sight awaited him. It was as though someone had placed the ancient cathedral before him covered in glittering gold, bright and translucent. Floodlights planted at the base of the magnificent home to God highlighted each nook and cranny, sand-yellow bricks slotting into each other, the curve of stone around its large circular window. All in golden light, pure and clean, weightlessly floating toward him. Breathtaking in its splendour.

How often had he remained in darkness, always too weak in spirit to open the shutter to let in the light... until now.

AUTHOR'S NOTE

*This story was voted the best by my team.
Lorie's illustration was breathtaking.
The story remained unplanned to the end.*

It was a laundry list of complaints, from trespassing into Spain, to arriving at a monochromatic hotel pestered by well-meaning collegiates—until I awoke in the middle of the night, couldn't find a light and opened the window...

Lo and Behold!

ILLUSTRATOR'S NOTE

No joy as glorious as the thrill of a sudden moment that pulls you completely out of disappointment or the mundane— into a soul-healing experience of incredible beauty.

CHAPTER 7

SKIRTING THE GHETTO

ROUND THE CORNER from Seville Cathedral, across a narrow-cobbled street, they dutifully followed Maria, their tour guide. Even at eight in the morning, he was sweating profusely from the heat and humidity of the Spanish summer at its fiercest. Wending their way toward what he presumed was The Royal Alcázars of Seville, the Caliph's palace, Maria halted abruptly and darted under an archway.

"We are now in the Judería."

"The what?" the boys echoed each other.

She smiled at their bewilderment. "This was the Jewish ghetto. Judería comes from Judea, their homeland."

The boys, tired and bored already, sore at being woken up so early on their holiday, demanded, "If this was a ghetto, why was it placed beside the palace? And across from the cathedral?"

Maria wasn't fazed at all. "Jews were prized for their mastery of healing, as well as their prowess in raising money for the Caliph and later for the Spaniards and their church. Interest and moneylending was forbidden for Muslims and Christians alike. These duties were delegated to the Jews, who had networks of moneymen across Europe."

Laura interrupted. "But the houses are immaculate."

"Times have changed. Today, these homes are priced beyond most peoples' budget. " That one there…" Maria pointed to one of a row of townhouses, all in sparkling white, stacked one against the other. "…sold for 1.5 million euros, around two-and-a-half million Canadian dollars."

He inspected the house with disbelief. It was no bigger than their home in Calgary, a mere 1,732 square feet. Where was the garage?

As if to shake the boys out of their funk, Maria turned Alex and Chris around by their shoulders. "See that house in its cul-de-sac? Notice the pretty, orange, brick-lined window? Below it a mosaic inscription? For almost three hundred years, the skull of La Susona, a Jewess, was nailed there."

The boys' faces turned grey. They bent forward, as though to throw up. This wasn't the best way to liven them up.

Maria observed their reaction with glee. "In the 1480s, the final years of the Jewish community in Seville, the Spanish Inquisition came to persecute the Jews." Maria glanced at her audience to make sure they were still listening. "Susona's father, don Diego Susón decided to rebel. The girl, infatuated with a young hidalgo, betrayed her father. He was arrested and burned at the stake. Susona lived the rest of her life in repentance. Jilted by her lover, left a pariah in her own community, Susona took to wandering the streets. Her dying wish was to have her skull nailed to the door of her home as a warning to others about the consequence of betrayal. Her skull hung there until the eighteenth century as a testament for her sin, her grief and the duplicity of Christians."

Laura shuddered, holding her hand over her mouth. Alex and Chris fidgeted on the spot, uncomfortable with the story.

Muslims from North Africa had conquered and held Spain for four hundred years. Under them, the Jews were treated with respect. Once the Muslims were vanquished by the Spaniards, Arab tolerance gave way to the Inquisition. Muslims who dared to remain were persecuted the same as the Jews. Mosques were desecrated and converted to churches and, until recently, their culture and heritage was shunned into oblivion.

The story was a poignant reminder to him of his immediate family's origin—a father born Muslim, brought up by Anglicans, a Catholic mother, and their baptised children. The Inquisition proved that racial prejudice was instigated by the elite of society—the educated and privileged.

In England, shorn from his own East Indian clan, he was brought up by a working-class English family who practised the Church of England faith with no real conviction. He lived with them in a council estate that, from all appearance to an outsider was but a ghetto of an impoverished, inarticulate breed of low-paid workers isolated in their own subsidised low-housing. To an outsider, Ellington Park smacked of neglect. To him it was home. His family instilled him with moral ethics: judge others by their character and actions, not by their social status; to do right by others, not take advantage of them; help those around you in every way you can—if you can't, don't get in their way. They taught him their work ethic—don't judge someone by the work they do, respect them for working. He had never seen any of his English family unemployed. No one applied for the dole. Along with values, they impregnated him with a working-class accent, impossible to expunge in the heady realm of middle-class accountancy he later pursued.

On his arrival in 1960, he was the only person of colour in the community of three hundred households. How could an alien break into their arcane domain? He loved to play football, going out of his way to join any street game he could find. At first, he was too exotic to allow in. He waited until the two sides were uneven in numbers, then asked again. Eventually, his persistence paid off.

"Wot's yer name?" they asked.

"Snow White," he always replied.

"Naw mate, wot's yer real name?"

His underweight body and low height left him grounded to the floor, allowing him to dribble past heavy-set defencemen in front of him to score time and time again. Years rolled by. More and more West Indians, East Indians and Africans infiltrated the community from far-flung reaches of the British Empire. At every break, his white teammates would complain to him about "all those bloody wogs and Pakis coming over here," never once paying any attention to his own colour. If a ruffian from a neighbouring estate harassed him, they beat up on him, warning him to "lay off our mate." To the average person, reference to wogs and Pakis was gross prejudice. To him, they had forgotten his origins completely, bringing him into their fold as an equal. It was the middle-class—the all so properly spoken, educated, and privileged that were the real chauvinists. Their eyes betrayed them each time. Despite their impeccable politeness, the colour of his skin, the accent of the ghetto would never allow him to penetrate their hallowed circle.

In Seville, the blazing sun began to take its toll. The temperature was now above 40°C. To combat the heat, the Arabs had built their streets narrow and winding to trap the cooler night air, releasing it gradually over the day. Canopies hung on either side of the streets to shelter pedestrians from the blazing sun. They were edged with plastic tubing of cool-running water. Perforations in the tubes let out mists of coolness. Still, he noticed Laura wilting under the pounding heat.

"Come, let's go indoors," enjoined Maria with her usual burst of enthusiasm. Her 'indoors' was a bell tower attached to the cathedral across the cobbled street. Thanks to Maria, they by-passed the queue of tourists almost encircling the church to enter the Giralda—"she who turns"—its named derived from the weather-vane, the Giradillo, perched three hundred feet high, soaring above the cathedral.

He stared up at it, his neck aching. "Maria, are we expected to climb all the way to the top?"

She smiled radiantly. "There are no steps."

"What do you mean?"

"If you look up the shaft, the way is an incline. This tower was once a minaret. A muezzin would have to climb to the top five times a day to call his congregation out to pray. The toil of climbing was less-ened with the use of a donkey to carry him up." She inspected him. "Would you like me to fetch you one?"

As the boys raced up the towers, he began to feel his age. But beside him, he saw men and women much older with walking sticks, shuf-fling past him.

Even indoors, the heat was stifling. All along the way up, the tower was pierced with narrow slits for defending archers in times of war. These could have introduced a welcoming breeze into the tower. Alas, visitors converged upon them like swarms of bees to a honey-comb, desperately squeezing their selfie-sticks precariously out of the openings to take whatever shots they could. The lack of steps made it impossible to take a rest in case you slipped and fell into the oncom-ing crowd below. Halfway, he spied a room with a large open slit to the outside. By a miracle, it was empty. He dashed in and sat on the slanted ledge. Laura and Maria joined him.

"Don't step on the donkey." Maria laughed.

"What donkey?" He looked around him guiltily.

"This was a resting room for it to catch its breath. Hay would be placed in a manger and water in a wide clay bowl to drink."

A moment's respite and they were off again. it took another forty minutes before they reached the top.

"Pops, what took you so long?" It was the angelic voice of Chris teasing him.

"Oi! Watch it, " he warned. If the kid hadn't been a foot taller than him, he would have tried his best to shove him over the parapet. After all, the kid was insured. He could use the benefit.

Maria took over again, showing them the whole city laid out beneath them: the bullring made famous in Carmen, the silver-grey Guadalquiver river which brought Seville its prosperity as a trade hub; the dodecagonal Torre del Oro built by the Arabs to guard the waterway—all under a cloudless azure sky. Soon it was time to descend to the cathedral, after Laura and the boys took their obligatory photos.

Like somnambulists they ventured into the sacred sanctuary. All thoughts of heat, aches and hunger vanished in the spectacular, mesmerising, homage to God the Almighty—which God was debatable. The Arabs took twenty years to build what transpired to be the largest mosque in the world, surpassing the Ayasofya in Istanbul in both size and splendour. On regaining their land, the Spaniards converted the mosque into the fourth largest cathedral in the world. As prejudiced as he was to the superiority of anything British, Westminster Abbey couldn't hold a candle to this mausoleum. Both enshrined the dead who had exalted their nation upon high. Here lay the tomb of Christopher Columbus held aloft by four kings of Spain: Castille, Aragon, Navara and Leon, captured mid-ceremony. Royalty interred here, included Ferdinand and Isabella who unified Spain under one kingdom and sponsored Columbus.

He found a nook in this pleasant cool oasis to sit down as the boys explored the innards of this vast enclave. Maria had taken Laura to where she could light a candle as an oblation. Despite the magnificence surrounding him, he could not ignore the cost of desecration to uphold its sovereignty. This had been a Muslim sanctuary dedicated to peace and holy observance. How many had been slaughtered in the taking of the Judería? He had witnessed the havoc and bloodshed wreaked upon its Jewish community. The Jews were given the choice to flee, be murdered, or converted to Catholicism. All this to sustain the marbled pomp and circumstance that surrounded him.

Prejudice manifests itself in all forms, be it by colour, creed, or action. On his first day at Griffiths, Miles & Sully, Chartered Accountants, he had innocently completed the Telegraph crossword puzzle while awaiting instructions—not knowing that to solve it was a ritual performed daily by the staff together on their arrival at work of a morning. As a result, he was resented by all.

Later that first day, as he twiddled his thumbs waiting for an assignment, Richard Norman, one of the two partners in the firm, walked in. "While you're waiting for work here, would you mind working in London for a week? We have an urgent audit to complete."

Would he mind? He jumped at the opportunity to dispense with these shockers and their arcane rituals.

"Report to Nizar at our London office. He'll fill you in. Oh," he hesitated for a moment, "pick up some luncheon vouchers from Pam, our secretary, for your meals. We'll reimburse you for your train fare when you're done. You'll be paid overtime for your travelling to London and back."

The London office was an old pied-a-terre in Farringdon. It was a sketch out of Dickens. Situated on the outskirts of the business district, the area exuded dirt and grime from every pore. A fog of exhaust fumes choked him. He climbed up a narrow stairwell to the second floor, crossed the landing and knocked on the door.

Nizar was the only inhabitant. He was a fellow Ismaili Muslim. Nizar had recently qualified as a Chartered Accountant, although he'd been with the firm for a decade, working at this office on his own, commuting daily from Hammersmith. The man was probably in his late thirties, chubby, with a round face, oversized black glasses and constantly snorting due to a bout of asthma. Nevertheless, his voice was gentle and accommodating. His first words of greeting were "Ya Ali Madut". Without thinking, he automatically replied "Mowla Ali Madat." "May the exalted Allah through Ali help you" and the response "May he help you too" were the standard greetings between Ismailis.

How did Nizar know he was an Ismaili? By his name? His features? His colour? The boys in Slough had ostracized him for completing a crossword puzzle. Nizar accepted him with open arms, assuming he was a practising Ismaili, never knowing he had spent twenty years away from his community, could barely understand a word of their language, let alone speak it. Wouldn't it be nice for once to be accepted for what he was, rather than what he appeared to be?

He was impatient to get started. Instead, Nizar sat him down, plugged in the kettle on the credenza behind him. There was no kitchen, only the one room and two small desks facing each other. A small narrow window let in the semblance of greenish, foggy light. The grime outside had entered within. The once-white stippled wallpaper, a remnant of the Victorian era, had turned a queasy brown. He smelt and breathed in dust, which had settled on almost every item in the room. While the kettle boiled away, Nizar extracted a round tin from his drawer. "Try these. My wife made them fresh this morning." They were diamond-shaped, orange-brown nut cakes. He hadn't eaten one for years. He was being led back to a life he had discarded aeons ago.

"What's this audit about?" he asked, once Nizar had poured spoons of sugar, thick condensed milk, then added cinnamon and nutmeg to the concoction, without asking. "Drink your Chai first. Enjoy the Jugu cake."

He imagined their destination to be a towering office block set in the heart of London—The London Metal Exchange, or some steel conglomerate.

"No, we're off to audit Missions Beyond. It's a Methodist charity operating out of their headquarters on Marylebone Road. I'll take you there, once you're done."

"But I thought we did commercial audits?"

"Those are Huw's, the other partner's clients. Richard deals with all the Methodist charities. They were handed down to him by his father, who was a partner before him."

The Methodist Centre was based in a large, marbled mausoleum of a building. They took the lift to the third floor where they were introduced to Janice, the head accountant. She seemed to have stepped out of an Alfred Hitchcock film. An elderly, white-haired lady with not a strand out of place, neatly dressed in a beige blouse and cardigan—she was the epitome of a gentlelady—the very picture of naive helpfulness. You were never sure if she'd end up being the murder victim or the murderer at the end.

"We send missionaries to places like Papua New Guinea and Borneo. Once, they were eaten alive and their heads shrunken by local tribesmen." Was she joking? Nonetheless, he was bowled over at the temerity to believe your faith should encompass all peoples including those whose lives and ways you could not comprehend, a million miles away from you.

They were led to a standard, spotless white, sterile office with a large window overlooking the main road clogged with traffic below. Tea—Earl Grey this time, not Chai—and fingers of homemade shortbread were offered and downed before they could start.

It was his first audit. "Nizar, why are these people so friendly? Aren't they scared of the audit?"

"We've done this every year at the same time for decades and found nothing. It's an annual formality. Why should they be scared? Janice has been here all her life and knows every transaction by heart. We never find anything out of place, but the audit has to be done to obtain a clean bill of health for them to raise money and apply for government grants. So, in a way they appreciate we're a help, not a hindrance to them."

Nizar was right. The books were meticulously handwritten and kept within an enormous black hide-bound ledger, seeming to date back to the time of David Livingstone. The work was no more daunting than the bookkeeping he had attempted to grasp at Hale & Co., his former masters in accounting. Here, all he had to do was tick and bob other people's work and get paid for it. Did he enjoy the work any better? Not really. Checking transactions to bank statements and individual donations to a register became a chore. But the redeeming factor was the interaction with clients. At his first job, he was closeted all day with a handful of articled clerks, writing up books of account. Here, he could wander around all he wanted, puff out his chest and command instant attention and conversation with anyone he wanted.

Within Seville's cathedral, he breathed in the cool air with grati-tude. Sweat had stopped running down his face. A calmness had descended. A few more minutes of tranquility to savour before his brood reappeared. Gazing around him at the grandiloquent artefacts and architecture, he couldn't help but ponder on the irony of Muslims being welcomed to audit the books of Christians, or prejudiced heathen cannibals secluded on a South Pacific Island, hunkered down at the foot of a bubbling volcano, their noses punc-tured with a protruding wishbone, waiting patiently for the arrival of a boatful of strangers... and their next meal.

AUTHOR'S NOTE

*Previously I had said the opening paragraphs of Passing
Through were my favourite pieces of writing.
I've changed my mind.*

*The best has to be the final paragraph of this chapter.
My accounting experience rolled out just as described,
as did my colleague along with a charity in existence for
centuries called "Regions Beyond Missionary Service"—
catering to a congregation of head-shrinking cannibals in
Papua New Guinea, with its calf-hide ledger containing
entries from the time of David Livingstone.*

ILLUSTRATOR'S NOTE

*Interweaving old prejudices with modern expectations—
while trying to parse out what is expedient in the moment
from what is just universal "human nature" expressing
itself in every culture and human heart.*

CHAPTER 8

SALAAM ALEIKUM

IT WAS A comfortable forty-five-minute ride on the high-speed Alta Velocidad Española (AVE) from Seville to Córdoba, at a comfortable time of day—11 a.m. The sun was shining. Farmhouses, herds of cattle, dappled horses grazing in brown, sun-baked fields flashed before his eyes as he glanced up from the chess board. The AVE had no time to dawdle or to allow its passengers to soak in the scenery. His eyes would begin to ache if he focussed for more than a minute on any passing object.

As usual, he was being trounced by Chris, who continued to coax more and more euros from his favourite mark—Dad.

"Pops, you were so close this time," Chris falsely encouraged. "You'll definitely win the next one. Let me set up the board again."

He prayed for a distraction from Laura or Alex, but they were engrossed in scrolling through their mail, oblivious to the world. Thankfully, before he could be hustled further, the trolley cart came to his rescue, full of free drinks and snacks—all part of their first-class compartment ticket.

Sandwiches never appealed to him. Instead, he grabbed a couple of packets of mixed nuts and biscuits for later, then studied the drinks. "What's that tall can? The one beside the Coke in a mosaic of colours?"

The server straightened his shoulders as though he had been waiting for this moment to show off his mastery of English. "It's mineral water from Catalonia. Vichy Catalan, naturally carbonated. The best in the world."

Best in the world? How could he refuse? Being a teetotaller, tired of Coke and ginger ale, worrying about his waistline, he had reverted to sipping mineral water whenever he could. The Vichy was delicious. It had a sky-high mineral content resulting in a zesty, salty after-taste. Before he could finish drinking, the AVE came to a halt, arriving at its destination without him losing another euro.

A few days earlier, on their way to Seville, they had stopped over at this station for an hour, waiting for a connection. The boys had rushed towards a packed McDonalds, taking Laura with them, while he took refuge in a local canteen. Córdoba station was built like a glass cathedral, far superior to any he had seen in rural England, and the place was swarming with tourists and locals alike. The major draw for these day-tripping tourists in their hundreds of thousands was the UNESCO World Heritage Site of the Mosque-Cathedral. His family was fortunate. They were here for three days to rest and recover.

To gain a taxi was an achievement in itself, much like at a major airport. Having queued for twenty minutes outside in the scalding heat, they sank gratefully into their seats, luxuriating in air-conditioned bliss.

"Hospes Palacio del Bailío, por favor," he articulated. There was a muffled answer from the orange-bereted cabbie. All he could make out was "Sí." With this, he had depleted his store of Spanish. His boys, who had spent a decade learning the language, provided no help. Even his Filipina wife, schooled in Spanish demurred to speak. In a panic, he ferreted through his backpack, pulled open the hotel confirmation and showed it to the driver. The taxi shot forward, as he, without the time to put on his safety belt, crashed his head against the windscreen.

The car was small, the size of a Toyota Corolla. While his family sat squeezed in the back, he racked his mind for phrases in Spanish. None came. He was now transfixed, staring out the window.

Twenty minutes passed and no sign of a hotel. This was all wrong. Like most European railway stations, Córdoba's should have been located in mid-town with their hotel a matter of minutes away. Laura tapped his shoulder, her look apprehensive.

Once again, he turned to the cabbie. "Where are we going? We passed a sign for downtown a few minutes ago. It was pointing the other way."

The man paid no attention. He was too busy weaving through the dense traffic at heart-pounding speed. Suddenly, the driver turned off the main road. Now they were climbing uphill along narrow, single-laned cobbled alleyways. Chris's nails clawed into him. Beads of anxious sweat dribbled down his forehead despite the air-conditioning. The higher they ascended, the less cars they saw. Shops were closed. Many were boarded up. Pedestrians had vanished.

"Stop! Where are you taking us?" He screamed at the driver.

The man's reply was totally muffled by an overgrown, thick, bushy, grey moustache, streaked with white that completely covered his mouth. What should he do? Without warning, the taxi lurched through a narrow white stone archway, halting in someone's courtyard.

The courtyard itself was paved in cobblestones. To the right stood, what appeared to be, stables constructed in heavy dark wood. To the left, a glass front ran from one end of the building to the other. A glass door automatically slid open. A bellboy appeared, loosened their bags from the cabbie's grip and guided them along the narrow corridor running parallel to the courtyard all the way to reception. The terminus was a low, two-desk affair. There was no grand entrance nor high counter. Was this the five-star boutique establishment so highly recommended by Joelle, their long-time travel agent?

What hit him was not what was there, but what wasn't. There was no hubbub, only an air of unhurried peace and tranquility. The corridor itself was lined with a long, low, pastel-white backless couch. At its side stood a five-foot-tall, earth-toned urn of ancient Etruscan origin. Save for the urn, every piece of furniture was brand new and spotless, all in white and tan. As his family were served cool, refreshing hibiscus juice, he handed over their passports and checked in.

It was 2 p.m. He addressed the girl assisting him. "We're hungry. Do you have a restaurant? Is it still open?"

The tiny girl looked like a junior high schooler. She raised her eyes from her laptop. "Yes, in the garden, round the corner. Here are your keys to suites 25 and 26 on the second floor. The bellman will take your luggage to your rooms while you eat."

Once again, he was awed by the stillness and the almost soporific pace of anyone he saw. Had they entered a cloister of avowed silence? There was no traffic. No noise, not even echoes from the outside. Quietude enough to drown you. The all-white calming corridor led to a glass double door with large, vertical, ornate brass handles. On exiting, they climbed down four white stone steps and entered a long, oblong garden where on one side stood a grove of orange trees. Underneath them were several small black wrought-iron tables and chairs, all unoccupied. On the other side, an infinity pool beckoned, adorned with green and white striped deck chairs. Between the pool and the end of the garden was a length of shallow water with fountains rising and spouting silently from it. As they approached, a waiter came to seat them at a table beneath the fragrant orange trees. He handed them menus.

"Would you like any drinks to start with?" the server asked almost in a whisper.

"Some Vichy Catalan, please."

The wisp of a smile from the waiter evaporated. "We don't serve any Catalan products here."

It was the start of the dichotomy they would experience across Spain. The constitutionally elected Catalan leaders were imprisoned for sedition. To him, coming from Canada, it was a rerun of Quebec's demand for independence.

They grasped their menus without a word. The usual "pub-fare" was on offer. Laura chose a Waldorf salad. Where did that come from on a pub menu? He followed the boys in ordering a hamburger and shoestring fries.

"Sir, the food will take at least twenty minutes. Each item is prepared from scratch. You will not be disappointed."

His eyes questioned Laura. She nodded.

As the boys extracted a pack of cards to play gin rummy. Laura fished out a guidebook on Córdoba from her voluminous handbag. He relaxed and drank in the garden. The gentle ebb and flow of water soothed his senses. The style was so Arabic. In 711 CE, desert nomads out of Africa conquered Spain and held it for four hundred years. Their greatest love was water. Wherever they settled, they created oases of serenity with pools, fountains, and gardens.

He too had once tasted peace and tranquility—as a child returning to Africa each summer from schooling in England—being led by his father's hand to prayer. Evening began with the rituals; the taking of a shower; the putting on of light grey cotton trousers and a freshly ironed powder-blue short-sleeved shirt, then the walk along the palm-fringed harbour as the sun set, before arriving at their mosque. At the entrance, they discarded their sandals, washed their feet to purify them then, step by step, they ascended the great wide marble staircase, softly exchanging "Salaam Aleikums" (Peace be upon you) with fellow worshippers, all friends or family in his tightly knit community, all gravitating to a large prayer hall above. Glassless filigreed windows lay open facing the ocean, allowing in the cool, salt-tanged breeze. As they sat cross-legged on freshly swept rush mats, a girl sang ginans, hymns of peace offering them solace. It seemed destiny had ordained him two lives, one after the other: one life to experience peace each evening cocooned within a girl's singing, followed by another, wandering the world to retrieve it.

In the garden of Bailío, Laura nudged him out of his reverie. The food was here. A half-inch thick, medium-rare burger was cooked precisely to his asking, slightly crunchy on the exterior and juicy within. Shredded onions along with mild spices had been added to the patty. The pungency of oregano stimulated his taste buds as he bit into the burger, its bun encrusted in poppy seeds, melting in his mouth. The burger surpassed any he had tasted. And no, the previous best had not been encountered in the heartland of America, but in England at a high-end "American" parlour. Shoestring fries, perfectly seasoned, were accompanied with homemade ketchup and authentic Dijon mustard. Curiosity seized him. Where did the buns come from?

"From Sevilla, specially baked for us and delivered fresh each morning. We are trying to earn a Michelin star, which is why we strive so hard. Our condiments are prepared in house too."

He discovered that the secret to excellence in cooking came from details such poppy seeds on the buns and not overwhelming the food with excessive ingredients.

Their burgers and fries devoured, the boys grew restive. Laura declared it siesta time.

"Go to your rooms and relax. I'll join you later. It's dessert time for me." He ended up with churros, fresh out of the oven, with thick hot chocolate to dip them in. The churros were oval shaped sticks of dough, six inches long with serrated edges, covered in golden castor sugar and cinnamon.

There was nothing more to do on a sun-baked afternoon. They would sleep and venture out in the late evening to enjoy some tapas as the locals did.

Alone for now, he had the luxury of exploring his temporary residence. The Bailío was a converted 15th century mansion built upon the ruins of a roman villa. No wonder it was so quiet. It only had a few dozen rooms. Half of them were vacant. In accordance with its unwritten rules, he crept along the corridor searching for any common room with an open door he could examine to discover its facilities. To his delight, he found one. The glass door opened into a large dining room. The ceiling was at least twenty feet high. It wasn't the ceiling he gaped at, but the floor. It was constructed of thick reinforced glass. Underneath that glass were the ruins of a Roman room, together with stone pillars that rose up to the glass floor. There were even coloured mosaics on the Roman floor. He couldn't wait to tell Laura and the boys.

Instead of taking the lift, he darted up the beautiful heavy dark wooden stairs. As he opened the door, he exclaimed. "Come with me. I have something spectacular to show you." Laura was fast asleep. He didn't have the heart to wake her. In his disappointment, he surveyed the room. The large open suite was bigger than any he had witnessed in Europe. There was no carpet, only a burnished wood floor. All was built with elegance and style. There were no plastic mouldings. He could jog from one end of the room to the other without bumping into any furniture. The space enhanced the room's tranquility.

Alright, he would take the boys down to share his find. Walking through their connecting door, they too were beyond waking. He returned to his room, undressed, and slipped into bed, falling asleep instantly.

His slumber was shattered by Laura insisting he wake up.

"What is it?' he murmured dreamily.

"It's past eight in the evening. Alex discovered a flamenco festival happening all night. We have to be at the plaza downtown as soon as possible to get a decent seat. Come on, get up. We have to go."

"But I want to show you this room I found."

"There's no time. You can show me in the morning."

A thud on the door. The boys barged in, riffling through his bag of goodies, biting into his favourite chocolate bars. "Come on Pops," they yammered, hauling him out of bed. "We have to go."

"Boys, there's this room I found. It must be a thousand years old."

"Sorry, Pops. We gotta go."

"And don't eat all your dad's snacks. You won't eat your supper."

He sighed to himself. No peace for the wicked. Gathering up his clothes, he had to put his sandals on in the lift to keep up.

Stopping at the concierge they asked, "How do we get to the main plaza for the festival?"

The balding, overweight man had trouble breathing. "We are on a hill overlooking the city," he wheezed. "As you leave the hotel, follow the road down. You'll reach the Plaza de las Tendillas. That's where the show is. You might be too late to get a seat."

They thanked him and rushed off.

As they clambered down the hill, every alleyway and street was ringing with Flamenco music. Each had its trio of performers— a man thrumming his guitar while a couple laboured to perform a Flamenco for the hundredth time. The couple wore their classic bright red and sombre black outfits. The girl sported a cordobés, a black wide-brimmed cowboy hat with a flat cap and strap.

Plaza de las Tendillas, the size of two football pitches, throbbed with spectators. At one end, an enormous stage with lighting equipment had been set up. Deafening music poured out, even though the perfor- mance hadn't started. By a miracle, they found a restaurant serving seafood tapas that gave them a table on the plaza with a clear view of the stage. The excitement infected his family. Too busy absorbing the scene, neither Chris nor Alex asked to play cards. The waiter chose tapas for them—clams for Laura and strips of fish inlaid with green olives and sweet peppers. Chris peeled the shells off large prawns, squirting lemon over the morsels. There was salad and rice blackened with ink from squids.

Performers began taking to the stage. Camera flashes came into action across the square. For a moment, there was a sudden hush. It was followed by a mighty roar for the stars of the show, who were obviously well-known and beloved by their audience.

As his family applauded with the rest of the crowd, his mind lingered on the peaceful afternoon spent in an Arab oasis of water and lawn, amid the fragrance of marmalade orange blossoms. Too long had his life been shackled to the endless bustle of daily living. Like a genie let loose from a bottle, an image rose before him of a girl singing plaintively in a marble hall covered in rush mats, its filigreed windows open to the ocean's calling.

AUTHOR'S NOTE

The tranquility of the Bailío entrances me still—and the contrasts and juxtapositions:

Eating a hamburger beneath an orangery, in a garden restaurant vying for a Michelin star. Its poppy seed bun delivered of a morning from 140 kms away, in a garden cultivated in the Arab manner, centuries away

A glass-topped cellar of an ancient roman home, replete with its original mosaics

The hotel, an island of peace in a sea of blaring clackety-clack of flamenco dancers for their annual all-night festival

That's travel!

ILLUSTRATOR'S NOTE

It isn't only trauma and dramatic events that shape a person's nature—just as important are the quiet and loving memories that inspire an intense longing to revisit or recreate moments of great peace and beauty.

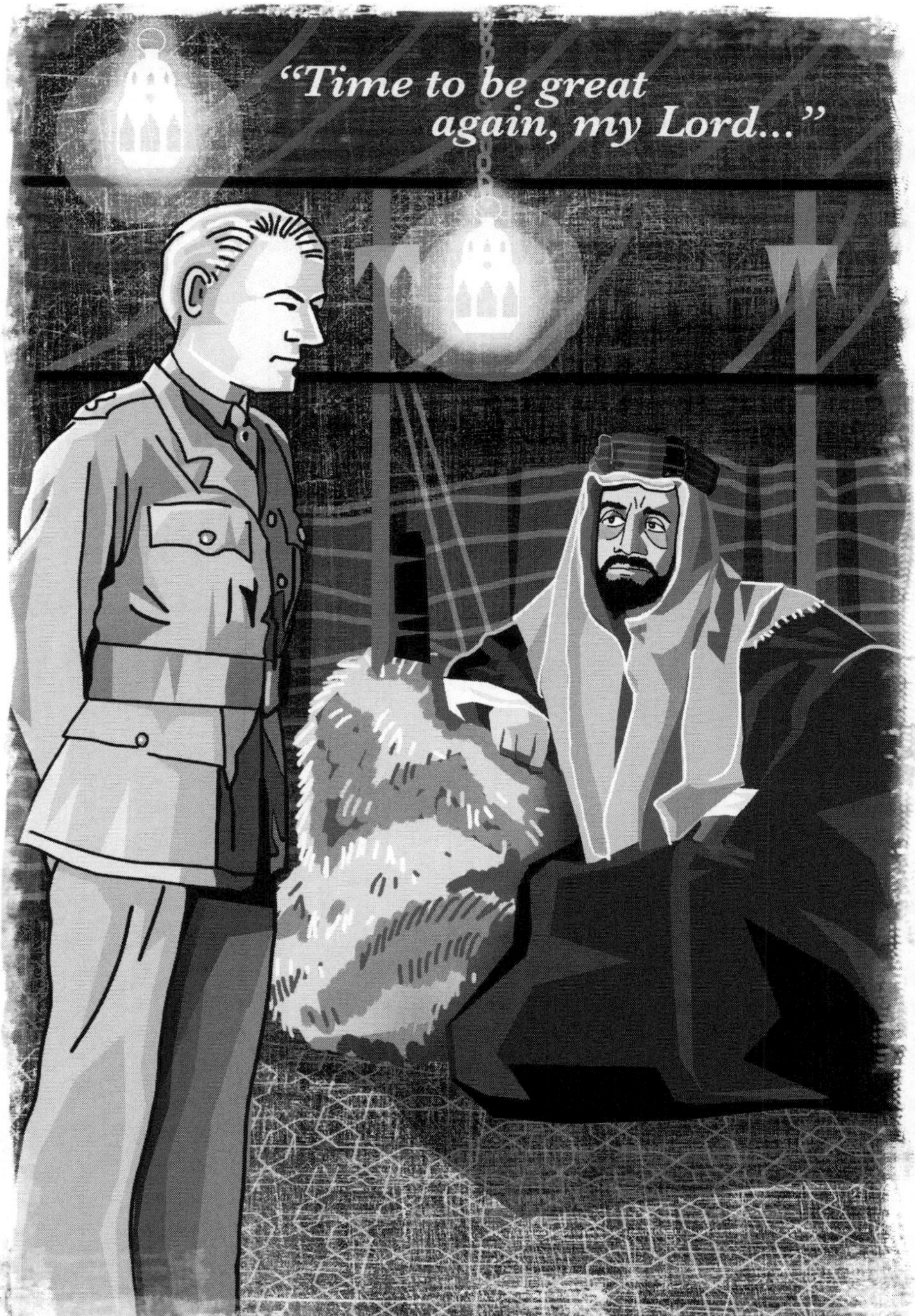
"Time to be great
again, my Lord..."

CHAPTER 9

THE VANISHED GARDENS OF CORDOVA

"HURRY UP!" he called out to them as they filed through the narrow, shaded Arab quarter. For once he was leading the charge. Laura and the boys sweltered in the heat—40°C, even in the shade. Sweating profusely under their baseball caps, they must have thought him mad, marching them at full pace when everyone else was taking a siesta. He couldn't help it. He was so excited.

Cordova. The name hung over him like rich, intoxicating Arab perfume. He had longed to visit her since a child. What would she be like? Were her gardens still abloom?

As he impatiently waited for his family to catch up he played back the image of a small boy, his head resting against his father's shoulder, watching wonder-eyed at the spectacle of Lawrence of Arabia on the big screen in Africa. The air-conditioning was full on at Chox, the newest cinema in town. Even now, he could smell the freshly roasted, salted peanuts he scoffed down out of newspaper cones and tasted the Canada Dry ginger ale, guzzled out of a forest-green bottle. His mind reeled from the scene that ignited his passion to visit and pay homage to this wondrous city and its revered gardens.

In the movie, Prince Feisal is assisting the British in their war against the Turks in Arabia during World War I. Feisal leads a tribe of Bedouins. His people are beggared, illiterate and lacking the most rudimentary weapons, wholly reliant on the meagre alms the British are willing to hand down to them.

Sitting cross-legged in his tent, Feisal laments, "But you know Lieutenant, in the Arab city of Cordova were two miles of public lighting in the streets when London was a village?"

"Yes, you were great," Lawrence admitted.

"Nine centuries ago."

"Time to be great again, my lord."

"My father is old and I..., I long for the vanished gardens of Cordova."

Why the emphasis on the gardens?

Shortly before seeing the movie with his dad, he had attended an obligatory religious class. There, an Arab missionary had proclaimed, "There is heaven on earth. It lies in the gardens of Cordova."

Arabs were desert-faring tribes. Their one love was for the scattered oases that gave them re spite from sand, heat and dust. They recreated their heaven in Cordova—a garden scented by exotic flowers, luxuriating amid pools of water.

The more he heard about the wondrous gardens, the more his imagination bloomed, strengthening his determination to see them for himself.

In 1960 he existed as the sole coloured person in a large, low-housing council estate in England. His working-class foster family and their neighbours still wallowed in the might and superiority of the British Empire. If you weren't English, you were inferior. Coming from Africa, you were tagged a "wog".

While the little boy in him didn't see it then, the grown-up understood the subconscious harm of relentless disrespect shown and the constant reinforcement of his inferiority. In the world he inhabited, no reference was made to a Muslim civilization nor of its worth. He had to hear it in a movie. Muslims were great... once. When London was a mere backwater, there existed a Muslim city that possessed street lighting. As he grew up, doubt niggled that Cordova, the once great capital of an Arab empire, still existed.

Cordova. The name spilled from his mouth like the bouquet of vintage wine.

Despite his desire to see this landmark for himself, he wanted to leave the Mezquita, the Alcazar and its gardens to the end of their visit. They took a couple of days pause in a boutique hotel at the edge of town, managing some desultory walks with visits to the occasional museum. Neither streets nor museums showed any sign or reference to ancient Arab street lighting. While the Arabs loved water and greenery—the Spanish converted them to cobblestoned plazas and courtyards.

Today, as they negotiated the narrow, winding streets, well before reaching their destination, they heard the tumult ahead. Abruptly, the narrow street widened onto a square, overwhelmed with sight-seers. It could have been any tourist trap in Europe. They battled through a surging tide of humanity toward the walled entrance of the Mezquita-Catedral.

A dozen gift shops peddling tawdry artefacts lined up for inspection. To each were attached sinewy queues of school-goers and elderly couples clutching each other for support. Ice cream parlours and snack bars were subjected to the same fate.

His family gingerly stepped over sticky chocolate wrappers, discarded chewing gum and plastic pop bottles. They vied for a foothold with streams of tourists desperate to keep up with their guides, who brandished pennants atop fully extended silvery car aerials that glistened in the sun. Guitar players strummed while perched upon discoloured brick embankments in front of the walled Mezquita. Chaos reigned, with neither dignity nor reverence for the third largest mosque in the world.

They trudged through a gated entrance to the Mezquita's forecourt. What had once been a lawn the size of a football field, raised six inches above the ground, was now mostly upturned rust-orange soil. With no sign to advise visitors to keep off the meagre grass, groups of students balanced on their haunches, huddled in small circles, twiddling with their phones. The lucky ones found shelter from the sun's grinding blaze under a handful of trees struggling to survive. The lineups were endless. Thank goodness he had purchased tickets in advance.

Laura and the boys didn't look well at all. Drooping from the perpetual enervating heat, they fell into a silent torpor.

From glaring sunlight, they entered cool refreshing shade. Hundreds of arches, nine feet tall, of beige and wine-red marble, loomed through the darkness at them. Each colour was layered one atop the other, transforming the arches into variegated stripes. Their splendour and excess spoke to the power of the Muslim Moors when Cordova (now called Córdoba) was their capital, from which they governed the bulk of Spain for centuries. In his pamphlet, an Arab scholar described the architecture as "countless pillars like rows of palm trees swaying in the oases of Syria." Even in the darkness, they took his breath away. The whole family stood transfixed.

Their commune was shattered by the howl of a child barging into them. Loud, brash voices echoed throughout this gigantic prayer hall, punctuated by the flash of cameras. The air in the hall was musty, its floor layered in dust.

In Africa, he accompanied his aunt each morning to market. On their way, they would tarry awhile at their mosque to make their obeisance. At that hour, rows of women volunteers, their backs hunched, swept clean the rush-matted marble floor—where were the sweepers today? This sacred place of worship was now transmuted into a theme park, with kids let rampant, treating it as their personal playground.

When the Spaniards recaptured their land, they obliterated all signs of Arabia until recent times. Mosques were converted to churches. Chapels were installed within the Mezquita, along with a cruciform nave and a transept. Observing the bloated crowd around him, this new-found Spanish enthusiasm for its Moorish past and its culture convinced him, more than ever, that it was a ploy to lure further visitors and their lucre to resuscitate the country's moribund economy.

He directed Laura to a place where she, as a practicing Catholic, could light a candle and dedicate a prayer. The boys were cut loose with their promise to return within half an hour. He was left alone to find his own place of belonging.

Peace was interrupted within minutes.

"Pops, Pops, come see this!" Invigorated by the cooler temperature indoors, the boys' voices shook with excitement.

They hauled him hurriedly to the other end of the Mezquita, to a lighted glass cabinet displaying cartouches—small tablets of sparkling white stone—each bearing the hallmark of master builders of this great edifice. Why this was so important to the boys, he couldn't fathom. Then it dawned on him. They had carved cartouches at school. The boys saw the Mezquita as just another ancient curiosity, with no visceral connection. The closest connection they felt was in their common experience with cartouches, while Laura was drawn directly to the chapels and offertories.

But what of himself? He saw the Mezquita as it should have been, a functioning mosque. He drew a comparison to his own mosque in Africa, where his community came to prayer and, in so doing, coalesced as one. Half a century on, it was still so alive to him. The Mezquita should have been more than a relict, swaying onlookers with its intrinsic beauty. It had been robbed of its spirituality.

They gathered up Laura, walked out of the entrance and on to the Alcazar—the caliph's palace and gardens. His footsteps slowed and shortened as they neared. They had passed through so much commercial detritus to get here, a glimpse of Heaven on Earth, vouched by chroniclers and poets of the ages. What would he find? His heartbeat quickened.

Another quote from Feisal came to him. "No Arab loves the desert. We love water and green trees. There is nothing in the desert. No man needs nothing."

The Alcazar was a stone's throw away from the Mezquita. In the past, a private covered walkway joined the two to provide shade for the caliph and his sultana as they walked to and from the Mezquita. Unlike the caliph, he and his family had no protection from the sun, contending themselves with a march across a square of hot cobblestones before arriving at its entrance.

The crowd thinned the closer they got. His thoughts drifted to the Alcazar's past that the boy in him had created. Where he had envisioned dozens of beggars sitting cross-legged in front of the entrance, beside vendors of sweetmeats, nuts and fruits, and sellers of exotic flowers, fragrant necklaces of jasmine and frangipani. Now he found only a bicycle rack installed by the entryway. A solitary man sold plastic bottles of filtered water out of steel buckets of ice for a euro. No beggars. No other vendors in sight. He inspected the ground before him—the rubbish, toffee wrappers and discarded ticket stubs had disappeared.

They entered through a narrow gate. One path led to the Alcazar, another to the gardens.

The grand Guadalquivir River flowed beside them, feeding three tiers of pools. On each side, shallow-curved, cream-tiled channels, barely a foot wide, continuously circulated water from one tier down to the next. In accordance with Arab custom, fountains spouted noiselessly. The lush gardens lay in stark contrast to the brown, bruised lawn before the Mezquita. Unlike the forecourt of the mosque, here the vegetation flourished. Hedges, plants, and magnificent pillar-sculptured cypress trees, thirty feet high, returned their gaze. A grid of boxwood provided the framework for a series of rose gardens.

The darkness of the Mezquita, its coloured arches faded with grime, was forgotten under the spell of roses exploding into colour—canary yellow, pale pink, carnation red, even powder blue. Their perfume hijacked his senses. Stock plants of variegated colours and hues imparted their own special odour akin to vanilla and cloves. Fewer visitors allowed the garden to retain its mystique. For a moment he closed his eyes, picturing the caliph and his bride, leisurely strolling through the gardens at twilight on their way to prayer, bathing in the prescient scents of Heaven on Earth.

Cordova. At last, he had found his home.

He turned around and froze in his tracks.

In the Muslim faith, no image of a mortal was allowed, but now—scarring the landscape—were statues of Spanish royalty. The Spanish had trampled over the sacrosanct. Included in the roster of statues, King Ferdinand stood before his Queen Isabella. It was here that Columbus had come to seek their audience to finance his journey to the New World. Their goal? To acquire even more wealth and power. As they had annihilated the Arabs, so they would go on to do the same to the grand and ancient civilizations of the Americas; to plunder lucre, not from common tourists, but gold, silver, and precious stones from the heart of sacred temples, destroying them all in the process.

Out of nowhere, he remembered the local bully from his council house days. "Oi! You wog. Go back home." He remembered his intimidation and the disrespect.

He looked back at the statues. The same mark of disrespect reflected off them. What had society learned in the centuries between those worldly royals and that illiterate bully? Where was the home he was supposed to go back to? As he watched Laura and his boys discussing the gardens—its roses and stock—he realized he had once again become a stranger in his own home.

What about his family?

Born in Canada, schooled in Canada, his boys had no doubt as to who they were or where they belonged. They were pukkah Canadians and Calgarians to boot. Each spring saw Laura return to her family in the Philippines for two months, to a home erected by her father before she was born, nestled among a brood of brothers, sisters, cousins, aunts, and uncles. Each year she organized reunions of her friends and classmates—those who had remained steadfastly at home and those who had succeeded in the New World. Now retired, they came home to renew their camaraderie.

The gardens were fast vanishing behind them as Laura gushed with enthusiasm over the flowers, their layout and care. "Boys, what shall we plant in OUR garden?" she asked.

AUTHOR'S NOTE

This chapter had to be the best, as it was the title to the book.
Was it the best? I can't judge.

What I remember most about this chapter was the toffee wrappers and dirt allowed to accumulate on the floor of the Mezquita-Catedral. Like all churches, our mosques were spotless with teams of volunteers cleaning the floors daily. Our mosques, the same as churches, permeated with a sense of peace and tranquility, not a circus of kids running around unharnessed as though it was a playground. There was no respect for this mosque and garden to which Muslims across the world once felt duty-bound to visit and pay homage as they do today to Mecca. Spanish authority had turned this into another money-grab opportunity from tourists.

ILLUSTRATOR'S NOTE

We see the person we aspire to be in our heroes. Impressions and dreams carried from childhood—whether from stories in a book, or flickering images on a screen, can indelibly mark someone's internal map of the world.

"*Perhaps some of them had also broken their fealty and emigrated...to provide their children with hope under an infinite sky.*"

CHAPTER 10

GATESHEAD REVISITED

"**WHERE ARE WE?**" he asked in bewilderment.

"Antequera," Laura answered." It's a town about an hour and a half from where we're going. They're building a high-speed rail. Unfortunately, for the time being, it stops here. We have to change to a local line to Granada. It won't take long."

The platform was glutted with humanity, the disembarking colliding with the embarking. All of a sudden, like a magic trick, they all disappeared—either onto the train or down the escalator to the welcoming, air-conditioned indoors. His family was left alone on the platform, eerily silent, that stretched into infinity.

He looked around to gain his bearings. They had been disgorged into an ultra-modern rail station resembling a gigantic spaceship, newly landed on alien soil.

"Pops, look behind you," the boys twittered." It's like being back home in the Rockies."

The snow-topped Sierra Nevada mountains rose above them in sharp contrast to the temperature of 40°C+ and the flat ground surrounding them—an uninhabited desert sprawled out before them with olive plantations in the far horizon. This vast area of virgin land to one side, the dominating range of mountains on the other emphasized how insignificant he and his family were.

With Laura tugging his arm, they escaped the heat and dust, descending into the heart of the station.

The fully air-conditioned main thoroughfare below reminded him of an airport terminal. Service booths and luggage check-ins stood at both ends of the building with visitor information, car hire firms and the like sandwiched in between. The enormous foyer was lit up with sunlight pouring in through large windows situated on all sides, just below the roof.

As Laura and the boys found a bench, he scudded across to a food counter. There, he loaded up with goodies in preparation for the final leg of their journey—freshly baked galletas, crunchy, milk-white cookies covered in muti-coloured sprinkles, petite, yellow-creamed horns and thick, steaming hot chocolate.

On arrival in Granada, they found themselves tumbled out of surreal Antequera and slap-bang into 19th century Europe. They and dozens of fellow passengers teemed out of the antiquated rail station. The modern steel and tinted glass of the Antequera station was replaced by crumbling stonework. They were told the station lay far from the city centre. They would need a taxi.

They emerged outside in sweat-inducing heat. It was afternoon, peak siesta time. Only one taxi stood available, its owner snoozing on the back seat. Suddenly a dozen passengers demanded his immediate service. On scooping up the first set of passengers, the cabbie promised to call in reinforcements.

An hour later, the four of them were stuffed into a taxi fit for two.

Their relief at being rescued from the all-consuming sun forbade any complaint of being packed like sardines in a tin, having to hold the rest of their luggage—too much for the trunk—between their knees and cradled on their laps.

A slew of derelict buildings met them on the way. Decay and despondency reigned supreme. All were in disrepair, boarded up. Graffiti was scrawled on the walls and on any unprotected windows. A lump came to his throat. He had seen it all before in the city of Gateshead in Northeast England. It was the same rot and decay which had impelled him to emigrate to Canada in 1980.

For several years, he trained as an accountant near London. Being the youngest company member, the newest and single, he was asked to audit a client in remote Gateshead. No one else wanted to go. "What? Leave our family for weeks on end to go to a mucky town in the middle of winter. You must be kidding. They don't even speak proper English. Good luck."

Spartan Redheugh was a steel manufacturing plant in its final death throes. Part of his assigned task there was to observe the annual stock count on December 31st. It required long hours in pelting rain and biting wind, observing the weighing, tagging and recording of countless slabs of metal.

Over the four years visiting Gateshead, he witnessed the slow grinding decay creeping into the community. Youths desperate to leave, their parents clinging to their jobs—their only lifeline to survival. And this was occurring all across the nation. If there was no hope for these people in a community they had lived in for centuries, what hope was there for him? What chance did he have of raising a family with a bright future for his kids? He too was liable to be laid off at the first sign of recession, once he was past his prime. The sheer hopelessness he witnessed laid the seeds in him to emigrate to Canada while he still could. In his last years working in Gateshead, he witnessed the boarded-up, graffiti-ridden storefronts with nothing to offer—

the same that he saw now in Granada. He wondered if the rest of the town would be as soulless.

His question was answered almost immediately—one minute they were driving through streets lined with derelict, lifeless buildings and then the next, through clean, smart, completely renovated shops and offices. What could possibly cause this sudden and dramatic change?

He had no time to ponder as the taxi came to a halt in front of the Hotel Palacio de Santa Paula.

The five-star establishment was squeezed and dwarfed between two buildings on the main Vía Colón. There was not an inch of space to separate them. Everything within the hotel was just as cramped. The lobby appeared to be sliced in half lengthwise with reception shoved into a corner. The first words he heard were "Sorry sir, we are fully booked. We can only afford you one room on the ground floor by the elevator. We have one other on the fourth floor, facing the rear." Laura and he preferred connecting suites. He sought Laura's approval. She only shrugged.

Santa Paula was originally a convent, hence its name. The hotel stood only five storeys high. Their fourth-floor room was shrouded in darkness. Black, wooden shutters had blocked out all sunlight to preserve the room's coolness. Once opened, they were treated to a sight out of the 16th century. Homes below them displayed dark, wine-red tiles on gently sloping roofs. Here and there, large, covered balconies sported washing hung on clotheslines to dry. It brought him back to the days of Gateshead, where his four-star hotel, catering to visiting affluent businessmen, flourished within an enclave of low rent housing. From that room in Gateshead, he too could see lines of clothing swaying in the wind—the denizens no different from the factory-reliant family living on the outskirts of London who fostered him.

It was in Gateshead that the contrast between the haves and have-nots battled within him. He remembered a similar late Thursday afternoon when he had been dropped off early from work by a company director in a Jaguar. Having time on his hands, he decided to bask in a bubble bath.

Growing up as a child in one of those low-rent homes, baths were limited to one a week on a Saturday. There was no tapped hot water for the bath. Water had to be boiled, then sloshed into a tub. The water barely covered his body as he lay down in it.

After luxuriating in the bubble bath that came to his chin while listening to the radio for an hour, he dressed, and went down to the restaurant where he perused the black, leather-bound menu. A Steak Diane would hit the spot, followed by Cherries Jubilee, flambéed on a trolley in front of him. He sipped red wine recommended by the sommelier. Nothing was too expensive. The client always footed the bill, and he was going to enjoy every bit of it.

His single, East Indian mother had forever dreamed of this lifestyle but never reached it. Juggling three jobs, seven days a week, she still managed to visit him regularly, haranguing him to complete his homework so he could enter university at Oxford or Cambridge and escape this council house estate. Yet he was content at Ellington Park Estate. He was now part of a family—a community that replaced the one in Africa his mother had wrenched him from.

It was in Gateshead where the two ideologies fought for his soul. His natural mother's unshakeable determination to gravitate to the top of society, to a life of privilege, warring with the dictum of his English foster mum, "Stick to your own kind and you won't be hurt"—her voice resounding in his head, as he wallowed more and more in luxury beyond expectation. Guilt reared its head. Somehow, he was betraying his own kind. But who were his own kind?

Their room at the Paula was small, though not uncomfortable. While providing all the amenities—TV, radio, all the plug-ins needed to charge Laura's devices (he never brought any himself)—no room was left for him to deposit his suitcase in a corner and have it open to riffle through, as was his wont. But the view from their window more than compensated.

A rap on the door announced the boys. Laura needn't have worried about being separated from them by three floors. They made themselves completely at home, requisitioning the queen-sized bed, raiding their poor father's goodie bag and flipping repeatedly through the TV channels, searching for a programme in English. Their parents were left to vie for the only chair in the room.

He marveled at his boys' aplomb, treating the Paula as home. They had taken to his mother's dream like ducks to water. He tried to detect any form of privilege or entitlement in them. There was none. The boys worked their hearts out at school, where they were highly competitive and successful. What touched him the most was their facility to not distinguish whom they met by their perceived status. They treated everyone equally. As his English mum would say "without airs and graces."

Eventually, he persuaded the boys to leave so he could take a nap and then meet them in the lobby at seven so they could eat.

"Hon, I feel like Chinese. Can you find us a restaurant?"

Having nothing else to do, he went down to the concierge to enquire about locating a Chinese restaurant—never expecting to find one. Europe wasn't like home in Calgary, Canada. There you could eat whatever you wished, from Uzbek to Indonesian. If you were in Spain, every restaurant served Spanish cuisine. The same applied to the rest of the continent.

The concierge crinkled his nose. "We have a district called Chinatown, five minutes away. Are you sure you wouldn't prefer Spanish? Our courtyard hosts an award-winning restaurant."

He answered half apologetically. "We've been eating Spanish all week. My wife is craving something different."

At seven, they crossed Vía Colón, walking two streets down as directed.

The wide, tree-lined boulevard was all aglitter with parading fashionistas. The main tourist sites—the Alhambra and Albaicín—were close by and packed with visitors. Granada's economy seemed to depend almost entirely on their activity. He found no other trade— as observed on their way from the train station. This pocket of affluence was isolated to the vicinity of their hotel.

Abruptly, they entered a dark alleyway. It appeared they had stepped into a foggy, 19th century dockyard area in London or Liverpool. Shadows loomed in and out of sight— ethereal, never concrete. The alley ended at the restaurant. Its windows were barred with deep red metal filigree. Heavy red and gold curtains prevented any peek within. He hesitated for a minute waiting for a go-ahead from Laura before heaving open the metal door. He glanced around. There were no customers.

A teenager in a silver and black cheongsam greeted them. "May I h...h...help you?" she stuttered in hardly recognizable English. Her appearance, her courage to speak despite a stutter, in what would have been a third language after Chinese and Spanish, filled him with admiration.

The dark, drab room was filled with shiny black-lacquered, traditionally carved chairs and tables. A large fish tank, set against a far wall, displayed tiny, blindingly colourful fish, the largest the size of his thumb, cavorting in its ocean of water. A faded painting of elderly Chinese men wearing hanfus, a girl in black, bathing beside a pool with mountains in the background, hung in desolate corners of the restaurant. The black, leather-bound menu was large—containing the usual suspects. It was bound in bright red cord.

Despite the grandeur and volume trumpeted in Chinese, Spanish and English, it listed the same dishes as an average restaurant in Calgary, which he described as "authentic Western-Chinese". Laura, in Filipina custom, ordered her staple diet of steamed rice, some salt and pepper seafood, a plate of thick Shanghai noodles with sliced beef and, for vegetables, Gai Lan in black bean sauce. The boys asked for sweet and sour basa fish with pineapple. While they were waiting for their meal, the waitress returned with a pot of scalding tea.

At the Restaurante Chino Estrella Oriental, the food arrived. It may have been pedestrian fare, but the oversized, overloaded plates were welcomed with delight. The boys dug in with gusto, as did Laura. Having eaten in full, his family still gobbling away, he called the waitress. He noticed not one other customer had entered all evening.

"How long have you been open?"

"My parents and I ca..ca..came from mainland China five years ago," she stuttered. "Mum and Dad can only speak Mandarin. While they cook, I serve. I'm their only child."

"You must be in high school?"

"Yes. I'm taking my finals this year."

"If you work here all day, when do you study?"

"We close at 9 p.m. I study while my parents clean up." He detected neither hesitation nor embarrassment in her, despite her perceived handicap.

He eyed her with growing admiration. But what was her ambition? Surely not to stay working at the Estrella all her life?

Her answer knocked him for six.

"I'm going to be a speech therapist. Help overcome their stuttering." With that, she headed back to the kitchen.

He stared at Laura, as if to say 'did you hear that?' She nodded. Imagine the odds the girl had overcome so far. Left her friends and community as a teenager, adapted to a totally alien culture, and learned a new language—Spanish. Then again, learned English as a third to help her parents' business. He couldn't help comparing her to his boys— happy in their own skin, motivated and confident, never mind industrious and ambitious.

Through the open kitchen door, he watched the girl's mother dicing vegetables, while her father sat on a plastic garden chair, in a stained white apron, reading a Chinese newspaper. They looked to be forty-ish. Why had they emigrated? Were they content, or only enduring this endless daily drudgery in a kitchen? Would they have left China if they had known their future? Perhaps they emigrated for the sake of their daughter—but how would the Estrella survive without her?

As an immigrant to Canada, he was fortunate. No alien language to contend with, met at the airport, accommodation awaiting him within walking distance of work, a well-paid, respectable career ahead of him. He was doubly fortunate to have a mother who re-fused to kowtow to her fate of marriage to "a bum". A mother who swore she would never allow her son to walk the path of his father.

As he paid the bill, complimenting the girl on the food, comment-ing on how much it was appreciated by his family, she asked, "Will you be returning here tomorrow? If so, please call us first to reserve a table. Here is our business card." She held the card with both hands, a sign of respect in Asia.

Was she serious? The place had been deserted all evening.

In explanation, the girl continued, "We have a booking for fifty people tomorrow night. A coachful of Chinese tourists. Perhaps twice a week they come. It's the only way we can survive."

"I'll bet you won't give them the same menu," he quipped.

"No sir. They won't eat from it. We prepare our own traditional dishes for them." He wasn't surprised. It was the same all over the world, including Calgary, where there was always a hint of an alternate menu—Chinese characters on a wallboard, their prices in English numerals, or a menu handed to him by mistake, completely in Chinese.

He took heed.

Stumbling through the unlit alleyway, his mind wandered back to the Geordies of Gateshead who he had deserted—holding on for dear life. What had become of them in the forty years since he qualified and fled to Canada… Perhaps some of them had also broken their fealty and emigrated to open restaurants abroad, to provide their children with hope under an infinite sky.

AUTHOR'S NOTE

Brought up by an impoverished working-class family in England, my heart went to the people and workers of Gateshead, experiencing the same threat of redundancy and hopelessness as my family was, at that time, during Margaret Thatcher's 'Winter of Discontent'. It was no help to be installed in a fancy 4-star hotel as I issued redundancy slips to workers, removing their last safety net, while the company directors grabbed lucrative settlements for their service.

The above was topped by the Chinese waitress who wouldn't allow stuttering to impede her dream of becoming a speech therapist to help others in a similar plight.

Like flowers squeezing out of cracks in concrete pavements, these small miracles are all there to witness, if we only open our eyes.

ILLUSTRATOR'S NOTE

*Some things are endemic to human nature and one of
them is seeking a better life for themselves, for their
family—making small changes in the traditional way they
were raised, or great adventures that lead them
to completely new horizons.*

"...they too yearned for the same respite from the heat..."

CHAPTER 11

IT'S ALRIGHT! HE'S FROM BARCELONA

TWO MORE DAYS before Barcelona. But first there was a double bumper of guided tours of Granada to shoulder. His family was tiring fast.

They began with the iconic Alhambra and its famous gardens. Far larger and grander than its counterpart in Córdoba, it still left him wanting. The historic site suffered the same malady that beset all Spanish homages to her former Arab masters. An overwhelming throng of tourists swarmed like mosquitos devouring a once bountiful crop. The painstakingly constructed harmony of red, sun-dried bricks of its outer walls and the palaces within, was torn asunder by the Spanish who promptly effaced the interiors, once the greatest salute to Muslim faith. Walls were pock-marked, where Arabic inscription had once existed in an artistic form of stone flowers. Christian crosses were superimposed upon Arab stars and crescents. Beautiful walls of filigree were sculptured into the shape of roses. Sunlight poured through gaping holes, the victim of Spanish cannon balls. His heart broke when he arrived at the centre of Alhambra. King Charles V had built a rotunda to compete with the finest Roman architecture of the time—the final desecration of the symmetry and beauty of Arab civilization.

During their stay in Granada, he felt he was participating in a charade for tourists. He never came close to understanding the locals, what they thought and believed in. Every act seemed a put-on to encourage visitors to spend their money, the denizens giving their guests whatever they thought was expected of them. For centuries, the Spanish had done their best to obliterate all trace of Arab culture—mosques desecrated, to be converted into churches and no Arab achievement celebrated, such as advances in medicine, mathematics, science, architecture, even poetry. Arabs gave Córdoba the first streetlights in Europe. No trace was found of those lights today—no plaques, no mention in any museum they toured. Granada's ghettos, on the way from the rail stations were conveniently hidden from the city centre, where tourists gathered, trapped in a bubble of false prosperity. Sadly, the mélange of high-end boutiques and premises were indistinguishable from any other part of tourist Europe. It amounted to an amorphous palate, to be savoured only by the rich who could afford it.

The second and final tour was of the Albaicín.

"Don't venture there alone," warned the guides. "It's the domain of gypsies and vagrants. The streets are dark and narrow. You could be mugged." They talked of the Albaicín as though it was a ghetto. No way did it resemble one. There was no tell-tale graffiti, nor houses of ill-repair, or anything resembling neglect. The cynic in him attributed these warnings to a ploy to create more work for the guides.

Picaresque Albaicín lay across the Darro River, running parallel to the Alhambra. This "dangerous" place reminded him of a wild animal defanged. Visitors milled its crowded streets constantly. A small, open-air market sold the usual gimcracks to doting tourists. From an open village square, the vista of Alhambra, with a backdrop of the Sierra Nevada mountains took his breath away. Apart from that one instant, the Albaicín filled him more with boredom than trepidation. It was all so quaint.

A language school stood in the centre of the neighbourhood. Minibuses laboured up and down the hillside community, morning, noon and night. Few homes were up for sale. Those that were, according to their obligatory guide, were scooped up for millions of ollars. So much for a vagrant's haunt. They passed houses, their bottoms painted sky-blue, their tops dazzling white—"blue to deter mosquitos, white to reflect the sun's heat away" explained their all-knowing, 200 euro an hour guide.

Parched tourists retreated into bars built into chalk caves, open all day to succour them. In the cooler evening, chairs and tables were evacuated out of the caves to the village square where Flamenco dancers performed under starlight, to the delight of their audience. Walking past a low brick wall, his heartbeat soared to a crescendo, when flames leapt up, almost engulfing him. It was a resident clearing his backyard of stubble.

It was time to go.

That night, as Laura packed her bags, she asked, "Hon, again, why is it we're going by plane instead of train?"

"Because it's quicker and cheaper."

He remembered his tussle with Joelle, his travel agent back home in Calgary, "Why fly, when we can take the train? Why use a low-budget airline? The last time we did so, the ground staff tagged our bags to a secondary airport outside Seattle, instead of Montreal. It took a week before we got them. I had to go to the airport daily. It ruined our vacation. And they charge extra for checking in that luggage. I've never had a budget flight that's left on time."

Joelle gradually persuaded him in her lowkey fashion. "The flight time is an hour. Your train time is eight. All trains run through Madrid, which means you're taking an L-shaped route, not a direct one." She glanced up at him to see if he was paying attention. "Can you imagine freeing up an extra day in Barcelona? Not to mention, the airfare is $100 per person, with no surcharge for your luggage. The train fare is double."

With a twinkle in her eye, she added, "The airline I've chosen, Vueling, is rated #1 in Europe for punctuality." Joelle had K.O.'d all his doubts.

The distance to Granada's mini airport was the same distance as to the railway station. There was no restriction on their luggage. The plane left and arrived on time. He sent a small prayer of thanks to Joelle.

Vueling was headquartered in Barcelona. It was owned and operated by Catalans. The airline's efficiency was the first indication of the professionalism practiced by them. It wasn't the way he was brought up to see them. Relaxed in his seat, his safety belt on, air-conditioning directed at him from an overhead jet, he recalled a TV comedy that epitomized the British opinion of a Catalan at that time.

Friday nights in England were for putting his feet up to watch Fawlty Towers. John Cleese played Basil, the owner, namesake and major-domo of a shambling British seaside home converted to a hotel. Andrew Sachs played Manuel, his batman, waiter and domestic. Anything that went wrong (and it always did) was blamed on Manuel, even though, for the most part, it was Basil who had blundered. Manuel could barely understand, let alone speak English. Basil would slap Manuel's head, wailing at his guests, "It's alright! He's from Barcelona." Today, the program would be banned for exhibiting extreme discrimination. But the comedy only extenuated the existing public opinion: Catalans were uneducated, inarticulate and incapable of performing the simplest of tasks. How wrong could they be?

Barcelona airport was a beauty to behold, new, shiny, and compact. It mirrored Vueling's business-like operation that had them exit within half-an-hour, their luggage intact.

On the way to their hotel, their taxi passed one gigantic sparkling-white residential block after another, all in excellent keep, no graffiti in sight. Almost every balcony vaunted a large bright yellow and red striped flag. "What is that?" he asked the cabbie.

"The Senyera, our flag of independence."

He had heard of the political strife caused in Spain by Catalonia wishing to break from the rest of the country. Recently, members of the regional government were jailed for wanting to hold a referendum to that effect. The whole business smacked of the fight in his own country, when Quebec fought to break from Canada. However, unlike Quebec's economic malaise as a result of this action, Barcelona's streets were lit up with prosperity, pride and confidence. The Manuel depicted on British television so many years ago, had transformed into a fashionable, energetic citizen of Barcelona, with a bounce in every step. After all, Barcelona was the capital city of Catalonia, the only place to live in. Did the impending threat of separation lead to a mass departure of business and individuals from Catalonia, slumping real estate prices, an air of malevolence toward the rest of Spain, similar to that of Quebec? Quite the opposite. The warm, brilliant sunshine reflected the composure of its people and the confidence of an endless stream of businesses migrating into the city and the autonomous community of Catalonia.

His family were offloaded at Le Meridien, at the upper reach of La Rambla. The street stretched for two miles, being the oldest and most revered in Barcelona. Its top end was chock-a-block with chichi stores found across the world, such as Mango and H&M. From there, the street drifted downward toward the harbour. At the bottom, La Rambla bifurcated. To one side, there was the old port with its myriad artisans selling beautiful, soft leather sandals, slippers and shoes, handbags, exquisite pottery and startlingly colourful tableware. Old Roman flagstone roadways were the order of the day. An ancient Roman cathedral stood guard over a dark charcoal-grey flagstone square. Houses of dark hewn stone rose several storeys high with gated courtyards, resembling, in his mind, a Roman colony. Where not privately occupied, they plied as museums or art galleries. An occasional café or restaurant cropped up.

In contrast, the modern harbour to the right displayed billion-dollar yachts owned by the wealthiest of the world, mainly Russian. A funicular gondola, under an azure sky, transported sightseers across the wide-open harbour, back to the city centre. The whole commotion could be savoured sitting outdoors on restaurant patios, sharing a bottle of plonk, nibbling tapas, being sheltered from the wind, noise and traffic by nine-foot-high plexiglass panels.

Le Meridien was the first prominent hostelry in Barcelona. Opera stars climbed the turret atop thereof and sang to their hearts' content, to be applauded by adoring fans below on La Rambla. The hotel may have dominated a loud, overcrowded street, but they were given two adjacent rooms facing the side street—a lot quieter and more peaceful.

The rooms were small, each with twin beds. Everything was off-white and old-fashioned, down to the delicate lace curtains, opening out to a quiet, tree-lined boulevard, akin to any in Paris. Apart from the twin beds, the room fitted Laura and him like a comfortable worn glove. There was an air of contentment. They lounged, unpacked, lounged again, gaining their breath back, all the while waiting for the boys to knock, enter and take over their room. The boys didn't appear. Perhaps they had found a favourite TV programme. Even now, in their teens, they loved to watch SpongeBob SquarePants wherever they went.

An hour passed; the phone rang. It was Alex. "Pops, can we go eat?

It's almost seven."

His eyes rested on Laura. "Yes. Come on over. I have the perfect restaurant."

Thirty minutes later, they joined the throng on La Rambla, making their way up to the Plaza de Catalunya. Thank heaven, the temperature was between 10 to 15C below other parts of Spain they had visited. This was because Barcelona lay on the Mediterranean, not inland. The city sat further north, inviting cooler air. The spicy aroma of sizzling donair meat one minute, freshly made waffles the next, enticed line-ups to form at their doors.

Why did this crowd draw him in, whereas Granada left him restless and wanting? Its citizens tried too hard to be what tourists expected Granada to be. In contrast, Catalans were comfortable in their own skin, confident enough to comport themselves naturally. Wealth, created by their own ingenuity, allowed them the luxury of not bending the knee to tourists. Like Parisians, Catalans celebrated their way of life daily. It began in the late evening sampling tapas from one bar to the next. Unlike Parisians, they welcomed the world to share their undisguised zest for living. Judging by the zillion nationals his family wended their way through, the world had taken up their offer with equal zest. The energy of the people was real and electric. Buskers, guitars in hand, sang mellifluously, urged on by onlookers who tarried a while, casting euro notes into their open musical cases. The outside patios of bars were full to bursting, their patrons challenging each other in animated conversation, as their hubbub and noise spilled onto the street. There was no sign of beleaguered parents dragging tired children from one stop to another. He could see no slouching, nor the weariness of a day's sightseeing and shopping. The animation in the open bars matched that on the street. All were determined to have a good time. He searched everywhere for the slow-witted, lampooned Manuel, the slap-stick butt to Basil Fawlty. Alas, he had long since vanished.

Plaza de Catalunya was a large garden, set on an oversized round-about at the top end of La Rambla. They crossed it to reach El Corte Inglés, a department store like Marks and Spencer or The Bay in Canada. It stood nine stories tall, with a restaurant on the top floor that doled out standard, bland canteen fare. So why had he brought them here? For the breathtaking panorama of Barcelona its wall-to-wall windows afforded. Plaza de Catalunya lay immediately below them, with its ornate fountains and statues. Hills etched the background. The bustling harbour and funicular gondola lay to their far left.

On the way back to Le Meridien, he felt a tug on his sleeve. "Pops, pops, look! An ice cream parlour. Can we go?" It was Chris, his younger son. They waited in line, the boys, having had their fill of food, were content to queue up, watching the street action around them. Laura took out her pocket guidebook, presumably planning for the next day. Three Saudi women stood in front of them. They were garbed from head-to-toe in deep black, traditional Muslim dress. Only the gold embroidery on their burqas, depicting scenes from their homeland betrayed their provenance. The women ordered Laura's favourite—pralines 'n' cream. As he observed his wife in a cool mandarin-orange T-shirt and custard-cream shorts, he marvelled at the heavy, pitch-black clothing of her counterparts and couldn't resist a smile. However ominous and alien the Saudi women appeared to be, they too yearned for the same respite from the heat and followed everyone else in line.

As he waited to be served, he pondered over the many contradictions he had observed on this first day. Barcelona, like any human being, possessed a multi-faceted personality. He weighed the dichotomy between Barcelona and Granada, the juxtaposition of the Catalan in reality compared to his portrayal in the British comedy show. He compared the optimism of Barcelona to the trouble and strife of a disintegrating Quebec. In his mind's eye he raised a toast to the

Manuel of Barcelona who robbed him of his Fawlty Towers image and enticed him to the night's throbbing 'Capital of the World'.

In the end, the observer chooses what he wishes to see.

AUTHOR'S NOTE

Being a lifelong devotee of Fawlty Towers, the title was fitting when writing about Barcelona.

The title also led to the underlying and barely noticed prejudice against foreigners and their English speech.

Like countless others, my heart went out to the Catalans and their magnificent, diverse city.

ILLUSTRATOR'S NOTE

When we stop making the choice to judge based on appearance, cultural differences and basic "otherness" and take down those barriers—we find our common ground and realize that sometimes (no matter who you are, or where you come from) you just want an ice cream on a really hot day!

"Pauper or king, we depart with nothing, but...
imagine the marvels we leave if we only dare."

CHAPTER 12

THANK YOU, GAUDI

A TRAM STRUCK him down one evening. No one recognized the old man in dishevelled clothing. As he had no identification papers on him, he was presumed to be homeless, taken to a paupers' hospice and left to die. On being given his final rites, he was recognized by the priest of Sagrada Familia. Antoni Gaudi was buried in the same church he had created—a monument as large as any cathedral in the world and just as famous. Citizens of Barcelona thronged to his funeral, paying homage to the most universal architect his city had ever known. It was June 10,1926.

Now, almost a century after his death, he had come across Gaudi, while riffling through a magazine in a dentist's waiting room and decided to plan a family trip to Barcelona. Why not spend a day walking in the footsteps of the great one?

The article piqued his interest beyond the Daliesque composition of his work—the self-absorption in his work to a point where what he wore didn't matter to him, the fierce patriot, never leaving

Barcelona, never accepting an assignment out of town, a foolhardiness to build an edifice which would take a hundred years and still be in the making, an absurdity of committing his all to a venture when he had neither funds nor the resources to build it. This was all at a time when Gaudi was comfortably off and able to accept generous commissions, refusing any that didn't interest him.

Why, at the peak of his career, take on an unheard-of costly project earning him nothing—one that would drag him down constantly, patching together piece-meal sums to continuously resuscitate his beloved vision?

Today, he and his family were ensconced in Le Méridien Hotel on La Rambla, at the heart of chic Barcelona. After breakfast, they sat in the lobby awaiting their personal tour guide.

"Pops," his boys chirped. "Why are we spending the day inspecting old buildings? There's so much else to see. Can't we go to the beach instead? What's so special about this 'Galfi', anyway?"

Laura wasn't much help, giving them a brief nod of approval. Before they could mutiny, Imogen, their guide, arrived. The bright, bouncy five-foot blond with a dazzling smile, raised his hopes until she reverted to a formulaic introduction—"Gaudi was born on June 25th, 1852. He was…"

Helplessly, he watched apathy creep into the faces of his family. Perhaps he had made a mistake in committing them to this tour. In their defense, how many times in his life, from primary school and up, had those words, "he was born…" sounded the death knell of an otherwise rewarding day. Yes, he was deeply curious to learn if the physical body of Gaudi's work matched the character and vision he had read about. But this conventional rote of facts dampened even his excitement and anticipation.

Noting their total lack of response, Imogen changed tack. "Before I take you to the Sagrada, which you are all longing to see, we'll go visit a park." She paused, waiting for a reaction. There was none. "To acquaint you with how we live, we will travel by public transport throughout."

He heard a sigh of resignation from his family. His heart sank. He had been so enamoured with Gaudi through his reading, he expected his excitement to rub off on Laura and his boys. It was too late to cancel the tour.

Leaving Le Méridien, they risked life and limb cutting through the crowd, then darting headlong into a subway. Despite being ten in the morning, well past any rush hour, the train was packed with tourists gabbling loudly in a dozen languages, gesticulating with one hand, carrying large, logo-plastered bags of merchandise in the other. Several stops later, his family were ushered out by Imogen.

On exiting, he was bitterly disappointed. A run-of-the-mill street rolled out in front of them—some townhouses, a couple of not-so-tall apartment buildings, a convenience store. No glamour whatsoever, let alone a statue, edifice or fountain. The architecture was completely devoid of character and grimy to boot. Where were Gaudi's buildings? Or were some of these his, so nondescript that they blended into the rest of the properties on the street? He feared the boys would be proved right after all.

Imogen directed them up some steps, then through a black, wrought-iron gate. A narrow, winding path led them steadily downhill. A concrete wall, six feet high, skirted the path on its periphery. The boys' eyes lit up. Brightly coloured shards of ceramics were embedded into the concrete. It was as if children had been invited to create artwork using broken, highly glazed crockery, marbles, and stained glass. He caught Laura smiling, hurriedly fishing out a camera from her voluminous handbag.

He neared the stonework, and gently caressed a bright blue, china saucer protruding from the wall. He was reminded of an afternoon, coming home early from work, joining Laura in the kitchen. Baby

Chris, unable to walk yet, was sitting down on the parquet floor, playing with a set of wooden bricks of variegated size, shape and colour. Chris was enchanted by them, particularly the blue ones. One minute, he would put a brick into his toothless mouth to explore its taste. The next, he would throw it, then crawl to retrieve it. His son now stood six feet tall, towering over him. He had all his teeth flashing as he too smiled.

His reverie was interrupted by Imogen. "The technique is called Trencadis, Catalan for broken up." She pointed at a corner. "They even use buttons and seashells. Look."

Running ahead, the boys were lost to them. He heard a whoop, not understanding why, until he turned the bend. A fantasy village greeted them. It was a cross between *One Thousand and One Nights* and *Grimm's Fairy Tales*.

Buildings sprang up in front of them, shapeless and lopsided. They appeared to be composed of fresh, still-drying mud, as though kids had been given giant buckets of Playdoh to create whatever pleased them. The roofs and walls were so misshapen, the mud appeared to be in motion, not quite solidified into static form. Some buildings boasted minarets, others grand, curving staircases to their door. Gigantic ceramic lizards with scaly textures appeared to slither out of their cave below ground. He observed all this as a child would on their first visit to Disneyland. Laura's reaction mirrored his own.

"This is Park Güell." Imogen declared. Her eyes lit up with mischief at the effect the park made on her guests. He couldn't hold back his enthusiasm either. This was exactly what he had wished for in Gaudi's creations. A few years ago, he had started to write. He too tried to instill a sense of wonder in his work. The joy of creating, which they both chased, was the creation itself in all its unlikely manifestation.

Once again, Laura seized her camera. She didn't know where or when to stop.

From his reading in Calgary, he learned on graduating that Gaudi's professor had remarked, "We have unleashed either a madman or a genius. Only time will tell."

Like Gaudi, he too faced life as an eccentric outsider. Despite being highly creative, through force of circumstance he enrolled into a highly conformist profession—an accountant in England. On qualifying, he escaped to Canada. There, like Gaudi, he eventually found his niche, creating tax structures for wealthy clients. As time progressed, he realized that also, like Gaudi, his purpose was to convince others to accept concepts beyond their own imagination—the power of ruthless creation.

Imogen continued, "Gaudi had many wealthy patrons who generously indulged his passion—Art Nouveau Catalan architecture. As a boy, Gaudi was sickly. He was forever taken to the countryside bordering Barcelona to recover. There, he fell in love with nature, later constructing mansions whose facades resembled trees in a forest, with animals peering through them. Gaudi read fairy tales, including *A Thousand and One Nights*, which introduced a Moorish influence to his work. This was reinforced by the actual architecture constructed by the Arabs when they ruled half of Spain, including Barcelona, for over four hundred years." She glanced at them to ensure they were listening.

He marvelled at Gaudi's determination to introduce fantasy and Moorish culture. How was he able to convince orthodox businessmen to accept his creations? And pay him well for them?

Their guide pressed on. "One of Gaudi's patrons, Eusebi Güell tasked him to create this park. It took fourteen years to complete. The Park won a UNESCO designation as a World Heritage Site."

How on earth could Gaudi convince a client to wait for fourteen years? His accountant's mind churned at the prohibitive cost of such a project. What magic did Gaudi possess to gain such licence?

"Seven of Gaudi's buildings, all in Barcelona, were awarded the same UNESCO designation. Gaudi never left Barcelona, refusing any assignments out of town. He was a true patriot."

Her words dealt a body blow to him. Due to political turmoil, he and his East Asian community had been forced to emigrate—he to England with his mother, while his father was left in Tanzania to salvage their assets in Africa. After a stay in England of twenty years, he once again emigrated, for economic reasons to Canada. Yet he still considered his home to be a serene bay on the coast of East Africa, with a promise, renewed each year, to return. How he envied Gaudi his determined patriotism.

The boys returned in time to be whisked through the exit to a regular bus stop—from the sublime to the normal. His mind teetered under the immense pull of Park Güell. He sat entranced beside the driver of a red double-decker bus, identical to those in London.

An old man wearing clothes from the 1940's came aboard. Despite the heat, he wore a grey woolen trench coat. A brown tartan, flat cap covered his head. His chin bore a week-old stubble. The man inevitably led him back to the article he had first read about Gaudi. In his accounting profession, he had spent a lifetime in formal suits and a buttoned-down personality. As he grew more successful he gained weight, along with a potbelly. He fell out of tight-fitting attire into looser casualwear, eventually turning to jogging pants and a hoody. By then, he was recognized for his talent and creativity within the business community, not by the clothes he wore.

Aboard the bus, he sensed they were nearing the Sagrada, "Imogen, why did Gaudi take on such a daunting task as this church?"

"Gaudi came from the working-class quarter of Barcelona, Dreta de l'Eixample, far from the opulence of La Rambla. Attaining prominence, he committed to erecting the Sagrada in his neighbourhood to create jobs for his impoverished community."

At the age of 60, the accountant decided he too wished to give back to society through writing. He used locals to edit, illustrate and book-bind his work. The project was a bottomless money pit. At his death, how would Gaudi have assessed himself? Would he have had an inkling of the astonishing fame and success of his Sagrada or chalk it up as a crushing setback?

The bus came to a halt.

They disembarked and stood to attention. The Sagrada caught their collective breath, holding it for some considerable time. Deemed Gothic, the architecture wasn't as flamboyant or grotesque as Park Güell, nor did it bow to the gravitas of feigned piety. Between the giant stork-like cranes, eleven spires shot up, with seven more to come, representing the twelve apostles, the Virgin Mary, the four Evangelists and, the tallest of them all, that of Jesus Christ.

Entering, they craned their necks to the roof, which hung 456 metres above them. Thankfully, Imogen let them wander on their own, while she took a break. "Get a feel of the place. Let's meet back here in thirty minutes. I'll answer all your questions then and point out some sights you may have missed."

The boys, of course, chose to climb the 504-step staircase to the roof. They sprinted up the first twenty steps and disappeared. Laura froze. Her hand clutched her heart. Imogen assured her, "The boys are quite safe. They'll learn to hold their palms against the enclosed walls, which form the innards of an enormous snail, in sync with Gaudi's whimsical melding of architecture and nature. The steps represent Christ's march to the cross."

Laura retired to the crypt to find Gaudi's tomb. Her husband remain-ed by the bronze, seven-metre high Door of Glory, fascinated by the Lord's Prayer etched upon it in more than fifty languages. At head height, he instantly recognized his childhood Swahili. Laura's Philippine Tagalog was close by. On a wall beside the door, his eyes fixed on a magic square—a series of numbers in four-by-four squares. Each row, column and diagonal added to 33, the age Jesus was believed to be crucified. Three is also the symbol of the Holy Trinity in Christendom.

In thirty minutes, the boys were back. "Wow! That was really cool. You should have seen the view from up there."

"Did you take pictures?" he asked.

"Yeah," answered Alex. "We've already forwarded them to our friends. We have a roaming plan." What they were spouting about, he had no idea. He had roamed enough for the day.

Laura swept up beside him. "Hon, look at the pictures I took."

Imogen recommenced her tour. Instead of dour looks, she was inundated with questions. Most came from the boys, with a sprinkling from Laura.

Hand-in-hand they walked together in awe between the pillars representing massive trees in a forest. Sunlight poured through stained glass windows onto the sparkling white marble floor. Each window reflected a different set of colours as the sun journeyed through the day, shining in from one to the next.

As they left, he mentally tipped his hat to Gaudi, reflecting that we enter the world with nothing, King or pauper, and we depart with nothing. But imagine the marvels we leave behind, if only we dare.

AUTHOR'S NOTE

It's now been seven long years of sweat and turmoil to stick to writing and publishing this, my third book.

Each time I lose hope, I think of Gaudi and—as I did in this chapter—tip my hat to his dedication to a project that, to the very time of his death, he regarded as a wasted failure.

Talking of death, what a way to open a chapter.

ILLUSTRATOR'S NOTE

Gaudi, a devout and driven man, spent his entire career creating a new lens to view architecture through. Perhaps he would have seen the lonely manner of his death as unimportant and the living legacy of his innovative, outstanding and uniquely personal work as all the recognition necessary.

CHAPTER 13

A PACKET OF TISSUES
FOR A GUCCI

THEY ARRIVED IN Serrano, a suburb of Madrid, shortly after 6 p.m. Their eight-hour train ride from Barcelona proved pleasantly relaxing but after a while, tedious. A taxi deposited them in front of a large ornate gate. Liveried men appeared out of nowhere, quickly taking charge of their luggage. They were guided across a cobbled courtyard, up some stone steps into what appeared to be someone's private study. It was as if he and his family had been welcomed into a stately home for a weekend retreat.

Their host sat behind a delicately carved, black-lacquered knee-hole desk. On seeing them, he stood up and ushered them across to a grand sitting room, with pastel-blue, oversized couches. They sank into large, plush cushions with matching pillows, grateful for the respite after such a long journey. Gilt-edged canvasses of bucolic, 18th century landscapes adorned the tall walls. No other guests were in sight. Not a hint of busyness like other hotels on their travels, only the impression of serene elegance. Even his chatty boys were lulled into silence.

"Welcome to Santo Mauro." Their host, attired in black formals examined their passports. Satisfied, he handed them back. "You'll be on the second floor in adjoining suites. Your bags are waiting for you there." The man pointed to a door to the left. "You will find a lift there if you don't wish to take the stairs."

The elevator was no more than a cubbyhole, barely large enough to hold one person, let alone luggage as well. He and Laura joined Alex and Chris to ascend the wide curved stairs to their rooms.

Painted the same baby-blue and white as the rest of the house, the rooms were spacious and sunlit. While Laura scurried around taking clothes out of her bag and hanging them in a closet, plugging in her electronic devices, he took time off to luxuriate on the bed, perusing the leather-bound folder outlining hotel facilities, a menu and map of the area.

Half an hour later, the boys entered, quiet and careful, as if not to disturb someone. "Pops," Alex whispered. "Did you know David Beckham stayed in our room for six months when he transferred to Real Madrid, down the road? There's a framed photo of him in our suite, along with the story."

"Then perhaps we should swap rooms," he commented mischievously. "Come, let's eat, Mum's starving."

They walked out of their hotel onto a wide, tree-lined boulevard. The neighbourhood easily competed with posh Kensington or Mayfair in London—large white stone mansions, greenery everywhere. Embassies, with square, highly polished brass plaques beside their entrances, indicating their hours of operation, were sprinkled among imposing private residences. The only thing missing were the usual crowds on these solitary streets.

A voice within him asked, "What are you doing here?" He longed for the council house estate in South England, where he was brought up. The rough-and-tumble of his down-at-heel community beckoned him still, after decades of absence. Serrano was all too neat and antiseptic. He had been the only coloured person living in the council estate when fostered by an Anglo-Saxon family. Somehow, he had managed to fit in. Looking around him, he doubted if he could be accepted here as one of its denizens—an East Indian and his Filipina wife would only be tolerated as visitors.

The idyllic image of perfection was dispelled by the sight of a lone African mendicant, plying his trade—the only non-white in the area, except for him and his family. He wondered how the man hadn't been jackbooted out as a vagrant. It reminded him that he too had once emigrated from Africa, a child in the arms of his single, penniless mother. How a family just as broke had welcomed him in, when his own mother couldn't feed him. Before he could investigate the man, they arrived at a tapas bar, and he was being pulled in by Laura and his boys.

Back at Santo Mauro, he and Laura bid the boys goodnight in front of their room. "Let's have a lie-in tomorrow, with a late breakfast and leave at noon," he suggested.

In their room, he watched Laura tidy up as he lay in bed. He flipped through TV channels looking to find BBC World Service but fell asleep with the remote still in his hand.

The next day at eleven, Alex phoned. "Pops, can Chris and I stay in, while you and Mum go out? There's a steam room and pool we want to try out. We need a break."

True—the family had been travelling now for three weeks. When taking them on a tour, he never wanted them to visit every significant site, but to leave the boys wanting to return when they left home and had a family of their own. That was why he always left a day or two between guided tours and made sure each never lasted more than half a day. If the boys asked for a break, they got it. At least they were independent and worldly enough to cope on their own. As a child, thanks to his dad working for an airline, he had travelled on his own since he was five, commuting between his estranged parents in England and Africa. At sixteen, he had made his first round-the-world trip, carrying a hundred pounds in his pocket to last him two months.

So it was—on a summer day—a husband and wife found them-selves strolling hand-in-hand down the main thoroughfare of Calle de Serrano. It was paradise resurrected for the pampered rich, an answer to Old Bond Street in London, or Fifth Avenue in New York. There were no pedestrian stores like H&M or Mango. Top-end haute couture and high-class artisanal boutiques were the order of the day. All there to cater to him and his ilk? But what was his ilk?

As he meandered through the luxury of Santo Mauro, wandering around the rich, sterile and patently safe area of Serrano, he noted it had taken the concerted labour of two generations (both on his and on Laura's side) for them to arrive here. His mother had worked her fingers to the bone, exhorting him to escape the tedium of manual drudgery and daily survival. He finally did. Laura's family eked a living out of the sugarcane trade on a minor Philippine island. Plummeting sugar prices wreaked havoc on their existence, leaving them with barely enough to eat. It was to secure college for her six siblings that Laura left home to work abroad as a nanny, despite her university degrees. Through her remittances, her siblings were ed-ucated to finally climb a rung above poverty.

Along Serrano they passed Hermès, where gossamer-thin silk scarves sold for 700 euros each. His foster parents would have choked at the price of such gimcrackery, considering it obscene. 700 euros was what their breadwinner earned in a month at a radio factory.

Next to Hermès, a window displayed a Kiton light-weight jacket for 4,000 euros. He stopped and examined it.

Laura blanched. "Hon, you're not buying that are you?"

He hesitated before replying. "No."

There was an ulterior motive to his evasiveness. Despite being surrounded by luxury, Laura still hadn't lost the sense of value she
had been brought up with. His foster mum would have applauded
her heartily, while his own mum would have told him to go get it, to
show the world they'd finally arrived at the head table.

As they proceeded, he became more and more convinced of the
superficiality of this whole district. It was all so deceptively perfect.
Even the in-store attendants wore haute couture, not to be surpassed
by their clients. Then, reality reared its ugly head…

Across the street stood the African, struggling to sell something to
no avail. Shoppers walking toward him suddenly executed a detour
around him, without stopping. Some were more annoyed at dirty-
ing their tanned, calf-leather shoes as they stepped onto the road to
avoid him.

There was no time to attend to the man.

He had found what he was searching for. In front of him stood a
Gucci store. On display was a sweater which he had seen in
a men's fashion magazine. It was dark blue with olive-green edging
and on it were columns of golden tiger heads.

He had never thought of buying presents for his kids just for the
sake of it. Nor did he practice the maxim of always buying equally for them. If he saw something for one, he bought it, without
a second thought for the other. Whereas Alex preferred simple
clothes of white, grey or black, Chris inherited his father's taste
for colour, flamboyance and quality.

"Chris will love it," he finally confided to Laura.

"You must be mad. It's 1,200 euros. How do you know it'll fit? Let's
bring him here tomorrow to see if he likes it."

He wouldn't budge, knowing full well that by tomorrow, she would have changed his mind.

Why did he persist? Since a child, he had scrutinized fashion magazines, falling in love with clothes they promoted. His foster parents could never afford to buy him anything other than leftover sales items from Oxford Street or knit him sweaters to wear. The white, cable knits were beautiful, but never the style he longed for. Now, finally when he could afford to, he was too heavy for the slim-fit garments touted by high fashion. Unlike their dad, both his boys were sinewy and six-feet tall—as handsome as models. If he couldn't wear the fashion, then why not have the pleasure of seeing Chris in them? Alex had no interest. With him, his father shared his love of books and art.

Finally, he had the sweater in his hands. He examined it carefully, falling for every detail. Then his eyes caught Laura looking at him, pleadingly. He could have sworn it was Flo, his English mum, peering at him. His mind seesawed between possessing something so heartachingly beautiful or foregoing an object that would be such anathema to those who loved him.

It must have been the fastest sale the young assistant had made in her life.

As they departed, he recognized an El Corte Inglés—the equivalent of an American Bloomingdale's—to purchase petite leather sandals for Laura. She refused. His shopping spree had unnerved her. Across the street, he sighted a Japanese ramen store. Laura's favourite dish was noodle soup, which they hadn't found since leaving Canada—anything to distract her.

The restaurant and its interior could have been located in any chic city in the world. The whole of Serrano could have been too. It was purposely built that way to attract the wealthy. Street names were oddly South American, such as Calle Caracas, a result of a syndicate of Venezuelan businessmen who developed the whole area.

On the way back to the hotel—laden with brand-name shopping bags, their stomachs full—he felt a tap on his shoulder. It was the African. Laura tugged at his arm to quickly walk away. He halted, curious to see what the man was selling. The African held out a pack of crumpled face tissues.

He spoke in perfect clipped English, "Sir, I am a refugee. Although allowed in, I have no work permit. Back home, I was a professor until my life was threatened. Instead of begging outright, I offer you these tissues as a token of my gratitude for your generous support. That's all I can do."

All of a sudden, in an instant, he was transported back to a previous life when he too was an immigrant, freshly out of Africa—begging to be fed, finding compassion from a family as poor as he was. Ashamed, he took the first euro note out of his pocket and handed it to the African, without a word.

His past came storming back. He weighed it against the hollow luxury of his present. What he would have given to be back in the arms of Flo, his foster mum, now long dead, along with the rest of her family. His eyes fell on the fabulous brand-name bags he carried. Would he give all this up to live his previous life? Without waiting for a thank you, he turned away, clutching Laura's hand as though he would never let go.

A peculiar question nagged him all the way back to the hotel. What if he had been offered a pack of crumpled tissues in exchange for a Gucci?

AUTHOR'S NOTE

*O my goodness! My heart (eventually) went out to this
poor migrant. But only in the end.*

*Until that time, I harboured safely behind my successful,
upper middle-class armour, observing this man come to haunt
us across Serrano. He was a nuisance just for being there
and forcing us to notice him.*

*Only in the nick of time, did I remember I too had once
been a penniless immigrant beseeching help—and how
blessed I was to receive it—from similar stock
of working-class poor.*

ILLUSTRATOR'S NOTE

*We've all been there—that annoyance at being
bothered by someone on the street, quickly (hopefully)
followed by shame and regret at our lack of empathy.*

*Everyone has a story and everyone is,
or was, somebody's child.*

CHAPTER 14

NESSUN DORMA

IT WAS THE beginning of the end.

Today was the last day of his family's holiday in Spain and, of their future trips together. A week before their vacation, he had driven Laura and Chris six hundred miles from their home in Calgary, Canada, to the west coast to attend Alex's graduation from the University of British Columbia (UBC) in Vancouver. Alex had immediately garnered a job in the same city, starting a few days from now. As a rookie, he was entitled to only two weeks of holiday per year. This kiboshed any future extended family get-togethers.

Two nights ago, they had arrived in Serrano, a suburb of Madrid, deciding to rest and recuperate before tackling its city centre. In hindsight this was a mistake. Their flight home was leaving first thing in the morning. This left them only a day to inspect a city, which should have taken at least three days to explore. His preference was to concentrate on one essential district, then come back to the hotel early to pack. He was outvoted. Laura and the boys wanted to cover every sight on their list. This meant, for the first time in all their travels, they would have to resort to what most tourists suffered—conflate three days of sightseeing into one, forced marching from one part of the city to the other.

A taxi collected them at 9 a.m., giving them enough time to both pack in case they were late coming back, and eat a generous breakfast to keep them fuelled for the day, but not so late as to run out of time. Twenty minutes later, they were dropped off half a block from the royal palace, the heart of medieval Madrid.

Walking down the main avenue—closed to traffic—he was delighted to come upon what appeared to be lifelike sculptures of a golden C-3PO accompanied by a silver robot. A knight in gleaming armour —sword raised high, about to deliver a death blow—stood beside an upright Christopher Columbus, both hands clutching the edge of a wooden table, poring over a map of the world. They were so realistic. As he took the lead, his family in tow, Laura shrieked. The knight was moving toward her, his sword whooshing through the air, as if to chop her head off. Seconds later, a cacophony of heavy metal music broke out from a boom box.

Next, C-3PO came to life, followed by the silver robot, all descending upon them. Abruptly, the knight lowered his sword, pointing it at a contribution plate at his feet. No sooner had they captivated his family, they froze in motion, the music silenced. It wasn't until he had deposited coins into their till, did they start again—only briefly—to acknowledge their thanks before fading out of action, to await their next set of donors.

Instead of comforting their mother, the boys hooted with laughter. It was the kind of prank they loved. On their first journey out of Canada, visiting Laura's family in the Philippines, they persuaded him to take them to a fairground. Both boys were too young to ride on their own. It was left to hapless Pops to accompany them. The trouble was,he suffered from acrophobia.

He slumped into a swaying chair, with a son tucked in on either side of him and promptly closed his eyes. "Tell me when we're back on the ground." A while later, the wheel came to a gentle stop. "Boys," he pleaded, "are we back on Earth?"

In a flash, they chorused, "Yes. You can open your eyes now." They were dangling at the highest point, where the contraption had stopped to gather its breath before descending. He felt like throwing up. Their laughter then was identical to the one they unleashed today on their poor, unsuspecting mother. Observing their mirth on one side, comforting a distraught Laura on the other side, a brief smile escaped him, to be quickly replaced by a scowl at his boys and a reprimand.

For the hundredth time, they entered a magnificent royal residence. Having decided in advance not to hire a guide, they waited in line to gain entry. He glanced anxiously at his watch. An hour lost. The whole of the royal palace and its cathedral were centred around a grand, cobblestoned square, the Plaza de la Armería. Facing them was the 2,800-room palace, only four storeys high, set across the entire length of the square before them, built on the grounds of a burnt down Muslim alcazar. To the left stood the Catedral de la Almundena.

Suffering from heartburn, he sat on a bench shaded by an awning to one side of the plaza, while his family explored. He hoped they wouldn't be too long. Alex was the first out. "Mum and Chris will be a WHILE. They're looking at costumes and jewelry." Son examined father." How's your stomach? Thought I'd keep you company."

"Lex, are you happy in Vancouver? Any chance of returning to Calgary? We miss you."

"Most of my friends from UBC are settling there. For the time being, I'll do the same. I'm thinking of moving to Paris next year, working for the Olympics. After that, perhaps the Maldives."

He had watched that quiet confidence and maturity grow in his son from a young age. Being born in early December, Alex entered school as the youngest in his class. Nonetheless, he easily made friends with those two grades above him. At the end of high school, one of them decided to study at UBC. He persuaded Alex to join him. They rented a basement in Marpole. Within six months, Alex's friend quit and returned to Calgary. But Alex stuck it out.

His reverie was interrupted by Laura and Chris plodding toward them through the crowd. The sightseeing and picture-taking over, he chivvied them away from the packed square, down the main, gently curving Calle de Bailén, several kilometres long, wending its way to the city centre.

Again, he checked his watch. It was mid-afternoon. A dozen sights still to visit. The merciless heat, dust and incessant squeeze of the horde had drained them. They were parched. Bailén was deserted, its inhabitants catching up on their siesta. Tall trees provided canopied havens from the brutal sun and a sporadic breeze cooled them down.

To Laura's great disappointment, the Basilica de San Francisco El Grande, grandest of Madrid's venerable churches was closed for the afternoon. He sighed with relief. An hour saved.

Their spirit sank farther under the oppressive heat, not knowing how long they had left to trudge to their next destination. Every shop was boarded shut. Not a soul in sight. Suddenly, Aladdin's cave opened before them. It may not have offered diamonds and rubies, but something infinitely more precious—water and sustenance. In the whole five kilometres of their trek, only this mom-and-pop store was open, soldiering on. The store was the size of a cubicle, barely enough room for them to walk through.

The entrance door stood open to catch any breeze it could—no airconditioning. The heat within, intolerable. An elderly Korean couple standing behind a makeshift counter gave them a weak smile. According to a sign stuck to the window, the store was open seven days a week, twelve hours a day. An aroma of ginger and garlic wafted throughout. He assumed it was the smell of cooking from the back of the premises, where the owners lived. They had left the door to their private quarters ajar. He sneaked a peek. Alex crept up behind.

"Pops," he whispered, "their home is no bigger than our garage." He appeared discomfited. "Imagine, that palace had 2,800 rooms. Bet half of them were empty. How can they allow an old couple to live like this? I couldn't take it for a week." Sweat was spreading across his forehead. In their extensive travels, they encountered injustice everywhere. Individuals, generally immigrants, running themselves into the ground to survive each day.

Within the labyrinth of the narrow, crooked passageways of the store, they discovered three slim coolers packed together, bearing ice-cold drinks. Shelves slumped, overburdened with candies and snacks. The boys grabbed packs of homemade fruit nougat and Laura, a cache of bottled water.

Out on the street again, a few more kilometres delivered them back to the city centre. A subway disgorged its passengers into them. Chris leapt toward a restaurant, pulling Laura by the hand. They hadn't eaten since breakfast. The place, a little grungy, was full of locals—workmen in yellow neon-taped jackets, their safety helmets dangling by their straps on the backs of their chairs—wizened old men absorbed in a game of cards and buxom matriarchs cackling to each other.

"Mum, they have seafood paella, but it's for two people. Can we share?" Chris—lanky and underweight—had been a fussy eater all his life...until they started travelling. Pops smiled to himself. This kid was now ordering rice brimming with clams, mussels, and squid, as though they were bosom friends. Twenty minutes later, a large battered, blackened pan, its fiery orange-yellow rice steaming and simmering, was thumped down in front of them, exuding the welcome fragrance of smokey fish competing with an abundance of spices.

Satiated, they continued their journey. Alex fished out a map, leading the way.

They entered a medieval world. The street narrowed. Tiny shops— centuries old— purveyed harnesses and ancillary equine paraphernalia. A baker invited them to purchase galettes—flat, round, open pastries topped with fresh sliced fruit. The aroma of just-baked bread was overpowering. His neighbour sold flags and heraldic pennons. Their path ended at the foot of a steep set of wide, stone steps.

"Lex, are you sure we're on the right road?"

"Of course," he replied without hesitation. Edited to here.

Several steps later, husband and wife were panting for breath. For a moment they stopped, gazed up longingly at their boys and exchanged a smile. Thirty years together, their communication verged on telepathy. "Once we had to hold their tiny hands to persuade them to climb. Look at them now." He squeezed his wife's hand.

At the top, a large ornate stone arch greeted them—the Puerto de Toledo—one of several gates converging onto Plaza Puerta del Sol, the grandest of Madrid's squares. Once again, the scene teemed with tourists. Everyone barged into the other. He constantly felt for his wallet. "Don't stay too long in the centre. Too many pickpockets," a friend had warned. He could well understand how easy it would be for a thief to prosper in this environment.

Plaza Puerto del Sol must have been a mile long. Statues, fountains and sightseers mingled into a confounding, bustling blur. Afterwards, all he could remember were the life-sized sculptures of Las

Meninas in every nook and corner. Beautifully formed women, with wide burgeoning dresses in brilliant, variegated colours. They were made of highly glazed porcelain, inspired by Velázquez's Ladies-in-Waiting portrait. This was the annual Las Meninas de Canido festival.

"Hon, can you take a picture of us please, beside one of them?" Laura asked.

Focusing the camera, the boys were taller than the six-foot manne-quin. In the middle, stood Laura. She was standing at their shoulder height. When they first began travelling, the boys had been waist-high to their parents. Would they ever have the chance of being together like this again? He imagined them married with kids of their own, inviting Mum and Pops to accompany them on their own family travels.

"Smile," he cajoled them. Laura could barely do so. She tried bravely, shoulders slumped. The boys, meanwhile, were full of pep and vinegar. There was a time when the boys were small and easily tired. Laura would carry the younger Chris in her arms, while the heavier Alex rested on Pops's shoulders, mussing his father's hair, like a mahout on an elephant, gently swaying from side to side. The hair had long disappeared, as had the parents' energy.

Pictures taken, the boys were on the run again. "Come on Pops, to the Prado Museum next." Alex once again took the lead, his broth-er matching him stride for stride. They dashed through the square as best as they could. Mercifully, the crowd thinned as they left the plaza.

Now Laura needed a break. The Westin Palace Hotel came into view. "Come. In there," he beckoned. They entered wearing shorts and dusty sandals, their T-shirts drenched in sweat, walking into the most luxurious, plush-carpeted, elegantly appointed reception, enquiring after a washroom.

There was neither embarrassment nor snootiness evinced by the staff, nor question asked if they were guests. "Down the corridor, sir." The wide baroque way led to a large rotunda, topped by a glass-stained dome. Beneath it hovered an exquisite crystal chandelier, sprouting a hundred candles. At its epicentre, the elite of Madrid society sat at a lavish brunch buffet, serenaded by opera stars. Every haute-couture piece of clothing, footwear, clutch bag, jewelry and million-dollar chronometer by Richard Mille was on display.

Yet, they were welcomed with open arms to join them. By his family's expectation, completely out of character. But, on every trip, there arrived this totally awe-struck moment—the priceless unexpected.

As they left, the final bars of *Nessun Dorma* rose to its crescendo. For the first time today, his family halted as one, swept away by the music—frozen in time.

Nessun Dorma. "Let no one sleep." All their past travels unrolled before him like a magic carpet. He'd watched his boys grow up, marvelling at the heights they had climbed. It was their last adventure together. He wished it would never end—that he would not surrender to sleep. For to sleep was to awaken back home, full of memories and nothing more.

AUTHOR'S NOTE

The agony and ecstasy of completing this final very personal chapter. Completed drafts range from four attempts to six. This chapter took eight.

The first draft began so well, that it looked like we'd have this wrapped up in two.

After gushing congratulations on such a fine first draft, Robin, my creative editor, turned on me.

"It's too busy. Like a laundry list of places visited, one after he other. There's NO emotional connection. The places and eminiscences don't fit. The beginning and end are fantastic. But the middle? Ugh!"

So it continued, forging its way through weeks of desperation—until finally—the book had its worthy finale

ILLUSTRATOR'S NOTE

"It ain't over till the fat lady sings..."

The curtain is falling on the last trip like this they will take as a family and this awe-inspiring moment sums it up in one lovely wistful "crescendo".

—THE END—

THE AUTHOR
Emil Rem

I WAS BORN in 1955 in Tanzania to East Indian, Muslim parents. My mother, who possessed no education but held impossible ambitions, divorced my father when I was five and was immediately ostracized by her community. She moved to England and took me with her. The only work she could get was as a trainee nurse, and she found she couldn't look after me. An English working class family volunteered to take me in until she could find a permanent home for me. The initial two weeks turned into 12 years before my mother took me away from them.

Father continued to work for an airline which permitted me to travel free on standby. Initially, the tickets were for visiting home every holiday I had. From the age of 12, I began to travel the world on my own. Neither of my parents could afford to come with me. My mother gave me a pittance for my travels— it was all she could afford. I would arrive at London airport with a carry-on bag and a wad of tickets and take whichever airline had space available. I could be in Moscow or Rio De Janiero, I never knew. Nor did my family.

With enough money to last me a week, I had little choice—either talk to the passengers and have them invite me to stay with them or sleep on the airport floor and walk to town and back. There were no guide books. I walked and walked until my thighs came to look like slabs of ham.

Travelling to Africa, I saw the gradual disintegration of my community as each country gained its independence.

In 1970, Idi Amin threw out our community overnight in Uganda and other countries followed suit, nationalizing businesses and property.

In England, my English family gave me a St. Christopher's Cross to protect me in my travels. Reaching Africa, the cross was replaced by a green armband of cotton thread and a Muslim missionary hired to knock some religion into me. But the harm had already been done. In England, the combination of school and joining the cubs for Sunday church, led me to fall in love with hymns and psalms and the beauty of prose in the St. James' version of the Bible. That, the learning of Christmas carols for the school play, and my teacher's Friday readings of *The Adventures of Tom Sawyer* or *Wind in the Willows*, brought on the love of literature. Books were an escape from the misery and solitude. Apart from my English family, they were the only stability in my life.

To spite my Indian mother who was always hovering around me demanding the best from me, I failed my exams and sped headlong into accounting to escape my mother's wrath and the threat to retake my final years at school.

My accounting qualification allowed me to make a new home in Calgary, Canada where I became a scourge to my employers— they found I couldn't add!

In Calgary, much to the distress of my mother, I married a Filipina who bore me two boys within 21 months of each other.
By mutual assent, both boys became Roman Catholic—leading
my mother to disinherit me.

My mother had always discouraged me from writing or anything
creative—there was no money in it. It was not until little by
little, as I heard of the death of 'this family member' or 'that
close family friend', that the thought came to me to preserve
these memories for my boys. My final decesion was precipitated
by the death of my father. He had joined us in Calgary several
years earlier and was beloved both by my wife and children.

THE TEAM...

LORIE MILLER HANSEN

I have been a professional graphic designer for over twenty years—but more importantly, I've been an illustrator my entire life. I began at the age of two, with an ink portrait of my mother on the front page of a very *very* expensive book. For someone whose passion is expression through art and creative design, being given the opportunity to work on *The Vanished Gardens of Cordova* has been an exciting continuation of my journey illustrating Emil's books.

My first drawing— I think Mom was impressed!

ANDREA CINNAMOND

In my former life I was a high-tech scientist, *then* I found the 'techy' online world where I could play at the intersection of logic and creativity—I was hooked. One of my many areas of expertise is the building and implementation of digital (ePub) books and I love nothing more (*other than my three teenagers and our cat Amesbury!*) than working with and supporting motivated, inspired writers and creatives. *The Vanished Gardens of Cordova* again employs all the book things I love—and really makes me want to go to Spain!

ROBIN van ECK

I am an editor and author of literary, contemporary, horror and weird, offbeat and creative nonfiction. *The Vanished Gardens of Cordova* (in its way) fits into all of those categories! It has been another wonderful project and one that has called on all of my editing skills.

 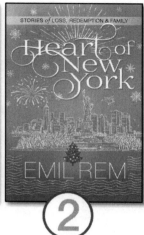 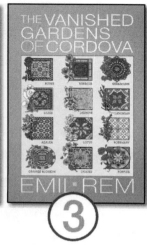

...BUT WAIT **THERE'S MORE!**

What is an **analect** anyway...

If you'd like to discover more of Emil's writing then go to **emilrem.ca/analects/** and sign up to receive his illustrated weekly (*usually!*) analects.

Alternately funny, heartfelt, insightful, tragic and "just because" ruminations on personal and/or timely world events...

Made in the USA
Middletown, DE
23 January 2024

48038042R00102